European
STUDIES

TONY WOODS
LIZ BIRD
MARIA WILLIAMS

Hodder & Stoughton
MEMBER OF THE HODDER HEADLINE GROUP

Cataloguing in Publication Data is available from the British Library

ISBN 0 340 56643 4

First published 1993
Impression number 10   9   8   7   6   5   4   3   2   1
Year   1998   1997   1996   1995   1994   1993

Typeset by Litho Link Ltd, Welshpool, Powys, Wales
Printed in Great Britain for Hodder & Stoughton Educational,
a division of Hodder Headline PLC, Mill Road, Dunton Green,
Sevenoaks, Kent TN13 2YA by Thomson Litho Ltd, East Kilbride

Contents

Preface

Attempting to write a book like this at a time of rapid change in the European Community has proved at best a headache and at worst a nightmare. Those foolish enough to attempt this task find themselves in an area of activity developing so rapidly on a variety of fronts that not only is it difficult to keep track of where and when these developments occur, it is almost equally difficult to collect all the necessary information and condense it into a manageable form.

Even as we write this preface, the Maastricht Treaty hangs in the balance: the debate continues in Westminster and the second Danish referendum is several weeks away. Eventually hard-pressed authors have to say: enough is enough; let's just say it as it is *today*.

The rewards of learning about Europe have been apparent to us and will, we hope, be so to the reader. Membership of the European Community affects an ever-increasing number of aspects of daily life: the goods available on the supermarket shelves, the standards of the products we buy, the conditions in which we work and the money we spend, to name just some of the most obvious. We know from contact with our own students that – encouraged, we hope, by us – young people are coming to regard themselves as citizens of Europe. Britain seems at last to have woken up to the need to learn European languages, and living and working in Europe is no longer the daunting prospect it might once have been. Even television soap operas see it as the norm!

There is still, however, a tendency, perhaps even reinforced by books like this, to think that Europe is 'over there'. The old joke headline 'Fog in Channel: Continent Isolated' is funny because its sentiment still persists, even in the outwardly Europeanized. Britain is and always has been part of Europe, economically, socially, culturally and psychologically. The long historical view supports this. We hope this book will encourage both younger and older readers to find out more about Europe and to remember that we don't go to Europe – we're in it.

It is customary for authors to use their preface to thank those who have helped them in their endeavour. Our families have put up with our absences, both mental and physical, while the book was being written. Our colleagues have been sounding-boards for some of the more esoteric bits of information. Our students have, as ever, been a source of inspiration, exasperation and delight. The silent angel has been Yvonne Gosling who has typed, retyped and, as always, never complained. Rowena Gaunt, Helen Coward and Gillian Bromley are those without whom this book would never have been completed and we thank them. Any errors are, of course, entirely our own.

Liz Bird
Maria Williams
Tony Woods

Hull, March 1993

part one

THE COUNTRIES OF THE EC

1
Country profiles

> **The tables in this chapter give, for each member state:**
> - Map
> - Key general information
> - Population profile
> - Economic profile
> - Political profile
> - International relations
> - Transport infrastructure
> - Communications

Introduction

The twelve member states of the Community vary widely in their geographical, political, economic and cultural characteristics. It is important to be aware of the key differences among them as these often lie behind differences in attitude to Community policies, both in individual policy areas and in terms of the overall scope and direction of the Community.

The 'big four' – Germany, France, Italy and the UK – are the most populous and industrially developed member states and arguably also the most influential in determining Community policy. Economically there is a clear division between these countries and the less populous, more agrarian-based countries of Portugal, Greece, and Ireland.

A further division can be noted between those who reject the concept of economic and political union, continuing to see the Community as little more than a free trade area (sometimes called 'minimalists') and those who believe that it has evolved beyond a mere trading bloc and must take the road towards full unity (sometimes called 'maximalists'). This division tends to range the earlier and later entrants against each other, with the founder members – France, Germany, the Benelux countries and Italy – showing more enthusiasm for the goals of economic and political union than some of the later entrants – notably the UK, Denmark and Portugal.

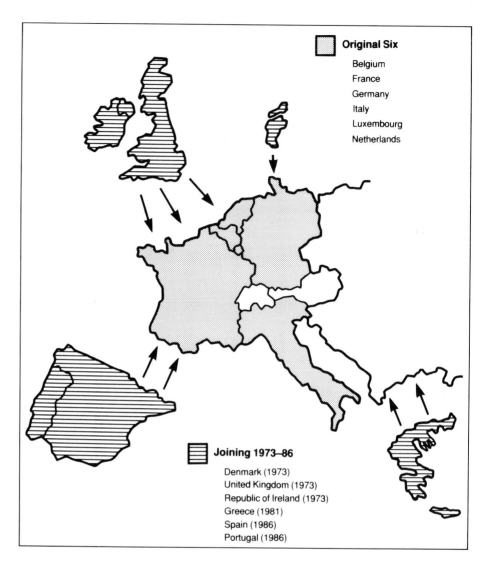

Original Six

Belgium
France
Germany
Italy
Luxembourg
Netherlands

Joining 1973–86

Denmark (1973)
United Kingdom (1973)
Republic of Ireland (1973)
Greece (1981)
Spain (1986)
Portugal (1986)

Figure 1.1 Map of Europe showing the original six members of the Community and the later entrants

These divisions are nevertheless over-simplifications and, while useful in identifying the kind of matters of concern to the various member states, must be examined in the context of more specific information, as well as in the light of historical experience. For example, while Italy has a strong rhetorical commitment to the European ideal, it has the worst record of any member state for ratifying Community legislation, whereas the UK and Denmark, despite their reservations about radical political developments, have the best!

The rest of this chapter consists of a snapshot of each member state in the form of a set of tables, allowing direct comparison of various features across countries.

THE MEMBER STATES OF THE EC

Belgium	(joined 1958)*
Denmark	(joined 1973)
France	(joined 1958)
Germany	(joined 1958)**
Greece	(joined 1981)
Ireland	(joined 1973)
Italy	(joined 1958)
Luxembourg	(joined 1958)*
Netherlands	(joined 1958)*
Portugal	(joined 1986)
Spain	(joined 1986)
United Kingdom	(joined 1973)

*Belgium, Luxembourg and the Netherlands are together called the Benelux countries, or just 'Benelux'.
**West Germany only until reunification in 1990.

A Guide to the Country Profiles

Each country section opens with a map. This is followed by the first table, which sets out some basic information about the country: its size (land area) and capital city; the currency used, language(s) spoken and religion(s) practised; and the head of state and current prime minister.

The *population profile* gives the size of the country's total population, the size of its active or working population, how this population relates to the size of the country and how it breaks down in terms of age.

ECONOMIC TERMS USED IN THE COUNTRY PROFILES

CIF   cost, insurance and freight
                *this means that the seller/exporter will pay for freight and
                insurance charges to a named port; all charges thereafter will
                be borne by the purchaser/importer*

FOB   free on board
                *this means that the seller/exporter is responsible for the costs of
                delivering goods to the ship, but all costs thereafter are borne
                by the purchaser/importer*

GNP   gross national product
                *the amount of goods and services a country produces,
                expressed in money terms and usually measured per year*

The *economic profile* gives basic information about the country's economic activity: its gross national product, largest companies, imports and exports, and the name of its central bank.

The *political profile* briefly describes the system of central and local government and outlines the results of the most recent elections.

Other tables then give information on the *transport infrastructure* – the size of road and rail networks, the names of national airlines – *communications* – details of the major broadcast and printed news media – and *international relations* – a list of the international organizations to which each country belongs (see box for abbreviations used).

INTERNATIONAL ORGANIZATIONS: ABBREVIATIONS USED IN THE COUNTRY PROFILES

EEA
*European Economic Area
an association between the EC and EFTA countries, focusing on free trade and certain aspects of the Single European Act (see chapters 3 and 7)

NATO
*North Atlantic Treaty Organization
an association, created in 1949, of Western countries dedicated to maintaining a single mutual defence system

OECD
*Organization for Economic Cooperation and Development
an organization formed to encourage growth and help stabilize exchange rates

Schengen Accord
an agreement among certain European states to lift border controls

UN
*United Nations
an association of states formed in 1945 to foster international peace and security

WEU
*Western European Union
an association of states formed in 1948, dedicated to collaboration on economic, social and cultural affairs and on joint self-defence

For more information on the role of European nations, and of the EC as a whole, in these international bodies, see chapter 9.

Belgium (Royaume de Belgique/Koninkrijk België)

Land area	30,518 sq. km
Capital	Brussels
Currency	Belgian franc (BFr) of 100 centimes
Languages	Dutch (Flemish) spoken in the north; French spoken by the Walloon south; some German spoken in the east
Religion	75% Roman Catholic
Head of State	King Albert II
Prime Minister	Jean-Luc Dehaene

Population Profile

Population (1991)	9,980,000
Active population (those in work or seeking work; 1990)	4,300,000

Population by age and sex (1988)

Age group	Total '000	Total %	Males '000	Males %	Females '000	Females %
0–4	580	5.9	297	3.0	282	2.9
5–14	1,223	12.4	626	6.3	597	6.0
15–24	1,475	14.9	752	7.6	722	7.3
25–44	2,918	29.5	1,486	15.0	1,432	14.5
45–64	2,263	22.9	1,105	11.2	1,158	11.7
65–74	779	7.9	341	3.5	438	4.4
75–84	512	5.2	180	1.8	331	3.5
85+	127	1.3	34	0.3	93	0.9
Total	9,876	100.0	4,822	48.7	5,054	51.2

Source: Institut National de Statistique.

Population per sq. km (1989)	326

Economic Profile

GNP per capita, US$ (1989)	16,390

Five biggest companies (1988)

Rank	Company	Sector	Market capital BFr bn	No. of employees
1	Petrofina	Petroleum	381.0	23,900
2	Société Générale de Belgique	General	274.5	–
3	Tractebel	Electricity/water	178.2	1,548
4	Solvay et Cie	Chemicals	168.7	44,301
5	Intercom	Electricity/water	146.2	8,558

Source: Financial Times Top 500.

Value of exports FOB, US$ bn (1989)	97.0
Value of imports CIF, US$ bn (1989)	99.5
Central bank	National Bank

Political Profile	
Constitution/ electoral system	Constitutional monarchy Chamber of Representatives (lower house) has 212 members, elected every four years on universal suffrage at age 18 Senate (upper house) has 105 members, two-thirds directly elected, one-third delegated from provincial councils
Local government	Belgium is divided into nine provinces and 589 communes. Communal councils are elected every six years. The president of the commune is the burgomaster and is assisted by aldermen.
Last election	November 1991
Results (seats in lower house)	Christian Social Party (CVP–PSC) 39 Socialist Party (FS) 35 Flemish Socialist Party (SP) 28 Liberal Party (PVV) 26 Liberal Reform Party (PRL) 20 Francophone Christian Social Party (PSC) 18 Vlaams Blok 12 Volksunie 10 Francophone Ecology Party 10 Flemish Ecology Party 7 Others 7

International Relations	
Belgium is a member of	UN, EC, NATO, OECD, WEU, Council of Europe, Schengen Accord

Transport Infrastructure	
Rail	Société Nationale des Chemins de Fers Belges (SNCB) 3,479 km of rail network (1991)
Road	1,631 km of motorways (1990) 3,970,317 private cars registered (1991)
Air	Main airline: Sabena; main airport National

Communications	
Newspapers	35 dailies, including *Le Drapeau Rouge* (communist), *Le Soir* (independent), *Het Laatste Nieuws* (independent liberal)
TV/Radio	Radio-Television belge de la Communauté française (RTBF) and Belgische Radio en Televisie (BRT) are public institutions

Denmark (Kongeriget Danmark)

Land area	43,093 sq. km
Capital	Copenhagen
Currency	Danish krone (DKr) of 100 øre
Language	Danish
Religion	97% Evangelical Lutheran
Head of State	Queen Margrethe II
Prime Minister	Poul Nyrup Rasmussen

Population Profile

Population (1991)	5,150,000
Active population (those in work or seeking work; 1990)	2,900,000

Population by age and sex (1989)

Age group	Total '000	%	Males '000	%	Females '000	%
0–2	171	3.3	88	1.7	83	1.6
3–6	212	4.1	108	2.1	104	2.0
7–13	435	8.5	222	4.3	213	4.2
14–18	219	4.3	113	2.2	107	2.1
17–19	219	4.3	115	2.2	106	2.1
20–24	414	8.1	213	4.1	201	3.9
25–59	2,413	47.0	1,223	23.8	1,190	23.2
60+	1,048	20.4	450	8.8	598	11.7
Total	5,130	100.0	2,528	49.2	2,602	50.8

Source: Statistical Yearbook.

Population per sq. km	119

Economic Profile

GNP per capita, US$ (1989)	20,510

Five biggest companies (1989)

Rank	Company	Sector	Turn-over DKr m	No. of employees
1	Det Ostasiatiske Kompagni	Shipping	17,791	15,197
2	FDB	Food chain	15,714	15,928
3	Post & Telegrafvasenet	PTT	11,934	33,894
4	MD Foods Amba	Dairy	11,280	5,517
5	Carlsberg A/S	Beverages	10,083	11,595

Source: Erhvervslivets ABC.

Value of exports FOB, US$ bn (1989)	31.3
Value of imports CIF, US$ bn (1989)	29.6
Central bank	National Bank

Political Profile	
Constitution/ electoral system	Constitutional monarchy
	Single-chamber parliament (Folketing) has 179 members, elected every 4 years by universal suffrage at age 18
Local government	275 municipalities (Kommuner), each with a district council of between 7 and 31 members and an elected mayor; 14 counties, each with county council and elected mayor. Local elections every four years.
	The Faroe Islands and Greenland are governed under a system of home rule
Last election	December 1990
Results (seats in Folketing)	Social Democratic Party 69
	Conservative People's Party 30
	Liberals 29
	Socialist People's Party 15
	Progress Party 12
	Centre Democrats 9
	Radical Liberals 7
	Christian People's Party 4
	Others 4

International Relations	
Denmark is a member of	UN, EC, NATO, OECD

Transport Infrastructure	
Rail	2,344 km of state rail network (1990)
	494 km of private railways
Road	601 km of motorways (1990)
	1,581,344 private cars registered (1988)
Air	Main airlines: Danair A/S, Scandinavian Airline System (SAS); main airport Kastrup, Copenhagen

Communications	
Newspapers	47 dailies with a weekly circulation of 1,810,000 (1990), including *BT* (tabloid), *Berlingske Tidende* (conservative), *Ekstra Bladet* (social liberal)
TV/Radio	Danmarks Radio and TV2 (state-owned)

France (République Française)

Land area	543,965 sq. km
Capital	Paris
Currency	Franc (FFr) of 100 centimes
Language	French
Religion	90% Roman Catholic
Head of State	President François Mitterrand
Prime Minister	Edouard Balladur

Population Profile

Population (1990)	56,600,000
Active population (those in work or seeking work; 1989)	24,400,000

Population by age and sex (1989)

Age group	Total '000	%	Males '000	%	Females '000	%
0–14	11,307	20.1	5,797	10.3	5,511	9.89
15–24	8,485	15.1	4,318	7.7	4,167	7.4
25–34	8,488	15.0	4,243	7.6	4,245	7.5
35–49	11,272	20.0	5,693	10.1	5,579	9.9
50–64	8,869	15.8	4,307	7.6	4,562	8.1
65+	7,882	14.0	3,080	5.5	4,802	8.5
Total	56,304	100.0	27,438	48.8	28,866	51.2

Source: INSEE.

Population per sq. km (1989)	103

Economic Profile

GNP per capita, US$ (1990)	17,830

Five biggest companies (1989)

Rank	Company	Sector	Turn-over FFr m	No. of employees
1	Renault	Automotive	161,438	181,715
2	PSA	Automotive	138,452	158,100
3	CGE	Electronic industry	127,958	204,100
4	Elf Aquitaine	Petroleum	126,097	72,200
5	Total CFP	Petroleum	83,290	41,862

Source: Expansion.

Value of exports FOB, US$ bn (1989)	185.3
Value of imports CIF, US$ bn (1989)	203.4
Central bank	Banque de France

Political Profile	
Constitution/ electoral system	Republic National Assembly (lower house) has 577 deputies, elected every five years by universal suffrage at age 18 Senate (upper house) has 319 senators, indirectly elected by electoral colleges in départements)
Local government	22 regions, each with directly elected regional council; regions made up of 96 départements and 36,551 communes. Each commune is run by an elected municipal council which elects its own mayor. The major represents both the commune and central government
Last election	March 1993

Results (seats in National Assembly)	Groupe Rassemblement pour la
	    République (RPR) 247
	Groupe Union pour la Democratie
	    Française (UDF) 213
	Socialists 54
	Other right 24
	Other left 10
	Left radicals 6

International Relations	
France is a member of	UN, EC, NATO, OECD, WEU, Council of Europe, Schengen Accord

Transport Infrastructure	
Rail	Société National des Chemins de Fer Français (SNCF)
	34,332 km of rail network (1990)
Road	6,680 km of motorways (1986)
	4,373,675 private vehicles registered (1986)
Air	Nine major airports; main airlines: Air France, UTA and Air Inter

Communications	
Newspapers	86 dailies with a circulation of 9,200,000 (1987), including *Le Figaro*, *France-Soir*, *Le Monde*, *L'Humanité*
TV/Radio	Two state-owned TV channels, Autenne 2 and FR3; five commercial TV channels; four main radio channels, France Info, France Inter, France Musique, France Cultur

Germany (Bundesrepublik Deutschland)

Land area	356,945 sq. km
Capital	Berlin
Currency	Deutschmark (DM) of 100 pfennig
Language	German
Religion	50% Protestant; 50% Roman Catholic
Head of State	President Richard Weiszäcker
Federal Chancellor	Helmut Kohl

Population Profile

Population (1990)	79,110,000
Active population (those in work or seeking work; 1991)	29,000,000

Population by age and sex (West Germany; 1988)

Age group	Total '000	%	Males '000	%	Females '000	%
0–4	3,147	5.1	1,616	2.6	1,531	2.5
5–9	3,037	4.9	1,558	2.5	1,479	2.4
10–14	2,940	4.8	1,510	2.4	1,430	2.3
15–24	9,193	14.9	4,709	7.6	4,484	7.3
25–34	9,747	15.8	4,995	8.1	4,752	7.7
35–44	8,048	13.0	4,096	6.6	3,952	6.4
45–54	9,184	14.9	4,699	7.6	4,485	7.3
55–64	6,903	11.2	3,265	5.3	3,638	5.9
65+	9,515	15.4	3,246	5.3	6,269	10.2
Total	61,715	100.0	29,693	48.1	32,022	51.9

Source: StBA Statistiches Jahrbuch 1990.

Population per sq. km (1990)	221.6

Economic Profile

GNP per capita, US$ (West Germany; 1989)	20,750

Five biggest companies (1989)

Rank	Company	Sector	Market capital DM m	No. of employees
1	Daimler-Benz	Automotive	40,519	338,749
2	Siemens	Electric Equip.	39,500	353,000
3	Allianz Holding	Insurance	39,194	41,752
4	Deutsche Bank	Commercial Bank	31,760	54,769
5	Bayer	Chemicals	25,962	165,700

Source: Financial Times Top 500.

Value of exports FOB, US$ bn (West Germany; 1990)	409.6
Value of imports CIF, US$ bn (West Germany; 1990)	344.4
Central bank	Bundesbank Federal Bank

Political Profile	
Constitution/ electoral system	Federal republic Bundestag (federal assembly; lower house) has 662 members, elected every four years by universal suffrage at age 18 Bundesrat (federal council; upper house) has 79 members, appointed by Länder governments)
Local governments	Germany consists of 16 Länder (states). Each Land has a constitution which complies with the federal Basic Law and has executive power within the Basic Law. There are 426 counties (Landkreise), 117 county boroughs (Kreisfreien Städte) and 16,127 communities (Gemeinden)
Last election	December 1990
Results (seats in Bundestag)	Social Democrats (SDP) 239 Christian Democrats (CDU) 268 Christian Social Union (CSU) 51 Free Democratic Party (FDP) 79 Greens 8 Party of Democratic Socialism (PDS) 17

International Relations	
Germany is a member of	UN, EC, NATO, OECD, WEU, Council of Europe, Schengen Accord

Transport Infrastructure	
Rail	The Deutsche Bundesbahn has been merged with the Deutsche Reichsbahn to give a rail network of 40,900 km
Road	11,000 km of *Autobahn* (1990) 35,500,000 cars registered (1990)
Air	Main airline: Lufthansa; eight major airports

Communications	
Newspapers	410 dailies with a circulation of 28,800,000 (1991), including *Die Welt, Frankfurter Allgemeine Zeitung, Bild*
TV/Radio	11 regional broadcasting corporations; two national television networks

Greece (Elliniki Dimokratia)

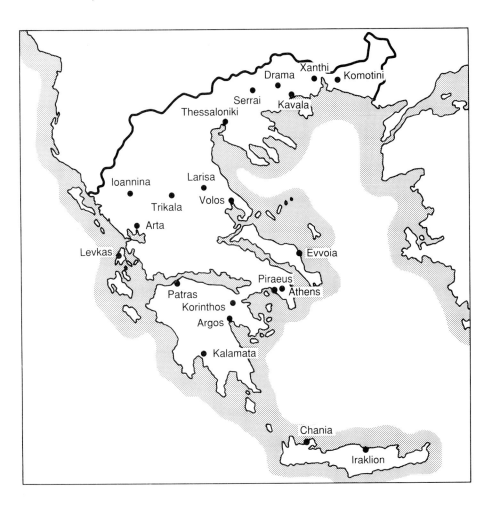

Land area	131,957 sq. km
Capital	Athens
Currency	Drachma (Dr)
Language	Greek
Religion	98% Christian Eastern Orthodox
Head of State	President Constantine Karamanlis
Prime Minister	Constantine Mitsotakis

Population Profile

Population (1991)	10,260,000
Active population (those in work or seeking work; 1989)	3,966,870

Population by age and sex (1988)

Age group	Total '000	Total %	Males '000	Males %	Females '000	Females %
0–4	574	5.7	297	3.0	278	2.8
5–9	701	7.0	363	3.6	339	3.4
10–14	705	7.0	365	3.6	340	3.4
15–24	1,491	14.9	771	7.7	721	7.2
25–34	1,397	14.0	707	7.1	690	6.9
35–44	1,303	13.0	649	6.5	654	6.5
45–54	1,252	12.5	596	6.0	656	6.6
55–64	1.215	12.1	578	5.8	637	6.4
65+	1,366	13.6	597	6.0	769	7.7
Total	10,004	100.0	4,922	49.2	5,082	50.8

Source: Statistical Yearbook of Greece.

Population per sq. km (1988)	75.5

Economic Profile

GNP per capita, US$ (1990)	5,758

Five biggest companies (1989)

Rank	Company	Net Income Dr 000	No. of employees
1	Duty Free Shops SA	4,296,647	489
2	Theocarakis, Nik	1,891,013	120
3	Toyota Hellas	1,851,033	220
4	Zampa SA	1,166,737	25
5	Philips	1,063,094	330

Note: Commercial companies only are ranked here by net income.
Sources: National Statistical Service of Greece, ICAP Hellas

Value of exports FOB, US$ bn (1989)	7.3
Value of imports CIF, US$ bn (1989)	14.3
Central bank	The Bank of Greece

Political Profile	
Constitution/ electoral system	Republic Single-chamber parliament (Vouli) of 300 members, elected every four years by universal suffrage at age 18
Local government	The republic is divided into 359 towns, 52 prefectures, 13 regions and 5,600 wards. The mayor is the recognized public figure in local government
Last election	April 1990
Results (seats in Vouli)	New Democracy — 152 Pasok (Pan Hellenic Socialist) — 124 Coalition of the Left and Progress — 21 Ecologist Alternatives — 1 Independents — 2

International Relations	
Greece is a member of	UN, EC, NATO, Council of Europe

Transport Infrastructure	
Rail	Hellenic Railways (OSE) has 2,479 km of rail track (1989)
Road	9,293 km of national roads (1988)
	1,729,683 cars registered (1988)
Air	Main airline: Olympic Airways; three major airports

Communications	
Newspapers	139 dailies (1988), including *Auriani, Ethnos, Ta Nea, To Vima*
TV/Radio	Hellenic National Radio and TV Institute is the government broadcasting station. There are three state-run and two commercial TV channels.

Ireland (Éire)

Land area	68,900 sq. km
Capital	Dublin
Currency	Irish pound (I£) or punt Éireannach of 100 pence
Languages	English, Gaelic
Religion	Roman Catholics 3.2 million; Protestant (Church of Ireland) 95,000
Head of State	President Mary Robinson
Prime Minister	Albert Reynolds

Population Profile

Population (1991)	3,520,000
Active population (those in work or seeking work; 1990)	1,305,000

Population by age and sex (1986)

Age group	Total '000	Total %	Males '000	Males %	Females '000	Females %
0–4	324	9.2	166	4.7	158	4.5
5–9	351	9.9	180	5.1	171	4.8
10–14	350	9.9	179	5.1	171	4.8
15–24	618	17.4	314	8.9	303	8.6
25–34	501	14.2	251	7.1	250	7.1
35–44	421	11.9	214	6.1	207	5.8
45–54	309	8.7	158	4.5	151	4.3
55–64	282	8.0	138	3.9	144	4.1
65+	384	10.9	169	4.8	216	6.1
Total	3,541	100.0	1,770	50.0	1,771	50.0

Source: Irish Central Statistics Office.

Population per sq. km (1989)	51

Economic Profile

GNP per capita, US$ (1990)	8,500

Five biggest companies (1990)

Rank	Company	Sector	Turn-over I£m	No. of employees
1	Jefferson Smurfit Group	Print and Packaging	1,661	15,825
2	CRH	Building materials	1,022	9,357
3	Digital Equipment International	Computers	965	1,600
4	Goodman International	Meat process/ export	926	2,514
5	An Bord Bainne Co-op	Dairy product export	893	1,200

Source: Irish Business, July 1990.

Value of exports FOB, US$ bn (1989)	22.2
Value of imports CIF, US$ bn (1989)	18.7
Central bank	The Central Bank

Political Profile	
Constitution/ electoral system	Republic Dáil Éireann (house of representatives; lower house) has 166 members, elected every five years by universal suffrage at age 18; Seanad Éireann (senate) has 60 members: 11 nominated by Prime Minister, six elected by universities, 43 elected from panels of candidates
Local government	Local authorities are elected every five years: 27 county councils, five county borough corporations; six borough corporations; 49 urban district councils; 26 boards of town commissioners. All local authorities have a dual management system, being run jointly by elected representatives, who are not salaried, and managers (paid officers)
Last election	November 1992
Results	Fianna Fail 68 Fine Gael 45 Labour 33 Progressive Democrats 10 Democratic Left 4 Others 6

International Relations	
Ireland is a member of	UN, EC, OECD, Council of Europe

Transport Infrastructure	
Rail	1,944 km of railways in 1989
Road	32 km of motorways (1991)
	796,408 cars registered (1991)
Air	Main airline Aer Lingus; two major airports

Communications	
Newspapers	7 dailies with a circulation of 648,000 (1992), including *Irish Independent, Irish Times, The Star*
TV/Radio	Radio Telefis Éireann

Italy (Repubblica Italiana)

Land area	301,277 sq. km
Capital	Rome
Currency	Lira (L)
Language	Italian
Religion	100% Roman Catholic
Head of State	President Oscar Luigi Scalfaro
Prime Minister	Carlo Ciampi

Population Profile

Population (1990)	57,700,000
Active population (those in work or seeking work; 1988)	22,800,000

Population by age and sex (1989)

Age group	Total '000	%	Males '000	%	Females '000	%
0–4	2,887	5.0	1,484	2.6	1,402	2.4
5–9	3,242	5.6	1,665	2.9	1,578	2.7
10–14	4,089	7.1	2,096	3.7	1,993	3.5
15–24	9,437	16.4	4,807	8.4	4,631	8.1
25–34	8,326	14.5	4,191	7.3	4,135	7.2
35–44	7,614	13.3	3,767	6.6	3,802	6.6
45–54	6,980	12.2	3,538	6.2	3,688	6.4
55–64	5,769	10.1	3,179	5.5	3,556	6.2
65+	5,388	9.4	3,162	5.5	3,679	6.4
Total	57,399	100.0	27,890	48.6	29,509	51.4

Source: Eurostat.

Population per sq. km (1989)	190

Economic Profile

GNP per capita, US$ (1989)	15,150

Five biggest companies (1989)

Rank	Company	Sector	Market capital L bn	No. of employees
1	Generali (Assicurazioni)	Insurance	32,540	–
2	Fiat	Automotive	27,538	277,353
3	Mediobanca	Finance	6,857	284
4	Montedison	Chemicals	6,701	47,115
5	La Fondiaria	Insurance	6,560	4,668

Source: Financial Times Top 500.

Value of exports FOB, US$ bn (1989)	149.1
Value of imports CIF, US$ bn (1989)	158.0
Central bank	The Bank of Italy

Political Profile	
Constitution/ electoral system	Republic
	Chamber of Deputies (lower house) has 630 members, elected every five years by universal suffrage at age 18
	Senate (upper house) has 315 members, elected by the regions
Local government	15 autonomous regions, plus five regions with special autonomy. Each has its own parliament (consiglio regionale) and government (giunta regionale e presidente). The powers wielded by these authorities vary from one region to another
Last election	April 1992
Results (seats in Chamber of Deputies)	Christian Democrats (DC) 206
	Communist Party (PdS) 107
	Socialist Party (PSU) 92
	Northern League 55
	Communist Refoundation (PRC) 35
	Italian Social Movement (MSI) 34
	Republican Party (PRI) 27
	Liberal Party (PLI) 17
	Green Party 16
	Others 41

International Relations	
Italy is a member of	UN, EC, NATO, WEU, Schengen Accord

Transport Infrastructure	
Rail	19,595 km of railways (1989)
Road	50,843 km of state roads and highways (1989)
	24,320,167 cars registered (1989)
Air	Main airline: Alitalia; six major airports

Communications	
Newspapers	73 dailies with a circulation of 6,005,000 (1989); including *Corriere della Serra, Il Giorno, L'Unità, Messagero, La Repubblica*
TV/Radio	Radiotelevisione Italiana

Luxembourg (Grand-Duché de Luxembourg)

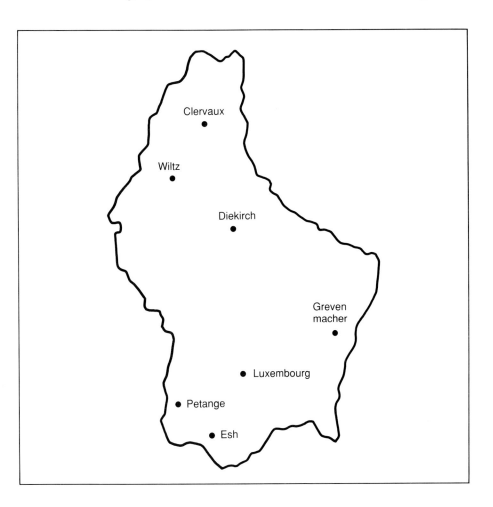

Land area	2,586 sq. km
Capital	Luxembourg
Currency	Luxembourg franc (LuxFr). Notes of the Belgian National Bank are legal tender in Luxembourg
Languages	French and German are official languages, as well as the national language of Luxembourgish
Religion	97% Roman Catholic
Head of State	Grand Duke Jean
Prime Minister	Jaques Santer

Population Profile

Population (1990)	378,400
Active population (those in work or seeking work; 1990)	162,000

Population by age and sex (1989)

Age group	Total '000	%	Males '000	%	Females '000	%
0–4	22,657	6.0	11,561	6.2	11,096	5.7
5–9	21,845	5.8	11,166	6.1	10,679	5.5
10–14	20,858	5.5	10,724	5.8	10,134	5.2
15–24	50,461	13.3	25,707	13.9	24,754	12.8
25–34	64,452	17.0	32,405	17.6	32,047	16.5
35–44	57,271	15.1	29,556	16.0	27,715	14.3
45–54	46,797	12.4	23,825	12.9	22,972	11.8
55–64	43,362	11.5	21,002	11.4	22,360	11.5
65+	50,697	13.4	18,614	10.1	32,083	16.6
Total	378,400	100	184,560	48.8	193,840	51.2

Source: STATEC

Population per sq. km (1989)	146

Economic Profile

GNP per capita, US$ (1989)	22,856

Five biggest companies (1989)

Rank	Company	Sector	No. of employees
1	ARBED SA	Steel	10,830
2	Goodyear	Tyres	4,090
3	CFL Luxembourg	Railway	3,660
4	Banque Internationale SA	Bank	2,150
5	Groupe Cactus	Supermarkets	2,070

Source: STATEC.

Value of exports FOB, US$ bn (1989)	186.4
Value of imports CIF, US$ bn (1989)	206.9
Central bank	The Monetary Institute

Political Profile	
Constitution/ electoral system	Constitutional monarchy
	Chamber of Deputies (lower house) has 60 members, elected every five years by universal suffrage at age 18;
	Council of State (upper house) has 21 members, chosen for life by the sovereign
Local government	Because of its small size, there are no rigid divisions between central and local government. There are four electoral districts
Last election	June 1989
Results (seats in Chamber of Deputies)	Christian Social (CSV) 22
	Socialists (POSL) 18
	Democrats (DP) 11
	Communists (KP) 1
	5/6 Action Committee 4
	Green Alternatives (GAP) 2
	Green Ecologists 2

International Relations	
Luxembourg is a member of	UN, EC, NATO, OECD, WEU, Council of Europe, Schengen Accord

Transport Infrastructure	
Rail	270 km of railways (1990)
Road	78 km of motorways (1989)
	183,404 cars registered (1990)
Air	Main airline Luxair; one major airport

Communications	
Newspapers	5 dailies with a circulation of 130,000 (1990); including *Luxembourg Wort*, *La Voix du Luxembourg*, *Super Lux-Post*
TV/Radio	Compagnie Luxembourgeoise de Télédiffusion

The Netherlands (Koninkrijk der Nederlanden)

Land area	41,864 sq. km
Capital	Amsterdam (seat of government; The Hague)
Currency	Guilder (Fl) of 100 cents
Language	Dutch
Religion	36% Roman Catholic; 27% Protestant; 4% other; 33% unaffiliated
Head of State	Queen Beatrix
Prime Minister	Ruud Lubbers

Population Profile

Population (1991)	15,001,000
Active population (those in work or seeking work; 1990)	6,000,000

Population by age and sex (1989)

Age group	Total '000	%	Males '000	%	Females '000	%
0–4	928	6.2	473	3.2	454	3.0
5–9	887	6.0	454	3.0	434	2.9
10–14	900	6.0	461	3.1	440	3.0
15–24	2,371	15.9	1,210	8.1	1,161	7.8
25–34	2,502	16.8	1,277	8.6	1,225	8.2
35–44	2,322	15.6	1,188	8.0	1,134	7.6
45–54	1,679	11.3	857	5.8	822	5.6
55–64	1,398	9.4	679	4.6	719	4.8
65+	1,906	12.8	760	5.1	1,146	7.7
Total	14,893	100.0	7,359	49.5	7,534	50.6

Source: CBS.

Population per sq. km (1989)	356

Economic Profile

GNP per capita, US$ (1989)	16,010

Five biggest companies (1988)

Rank	Company	Sector	Turn-over Fl m	No. of employees
1	Shell Group	Chemical/oil	154,450	134,000
2	Unilever	Conglomerate	61,961	295,000
3	Philips	Computers, h/hold appliances	56,079	310,000
4	AKZO	Chemical	16,581	71,100
5	Ahold	Retail	14,638	49,520

Source: De Omzetcijfers van 1988/Het Financieele Dagblad.

Value of exports FOB, US$ bn (1989)	115.7
Value of imports CIF, US$ bn (1989)	112.2
Central bank	The Netherlands Bank

Political Profile	
Constitution/ electoral system	Constitutional monarchy
	Second Chamber has 150 deputies, elected every four years by universal suffrage at age 18
	Upper or First Chamber has 75 members, elected indirectly by provincial councils
Local government	12 provinces consisting of 647 municipalities.
Last election	November 1989 (Second Chamber)
Results (seats in Second Chamber)	Christian Democratic Alliance (CDA) 54
	Labour Party (PvdA) 49
	Peoples' Party for Freedom and Democracy (VVD) 22
	Democrats '66 (D66) 12
	Green Left 6
	Calvinist Party (SGP) 3
	Calvinist Political Union (GPV) 2
	Evangelical Political Federation (RPF) 1
	Centre Democrats 1

International Relations	
The Netherlands is a member of	UN, EC, NATO, OECD, WEU, Council of Europe, Schengen Accord

Transport Infrastructure	
Rail	NV Nederlandse Spoorwegen 2,828 km of railways (1989)
Road	2,060 km of motorways (1988) 5,600,000 cars registered (1991)
Air	Main airline: Royal Dutch Airlines (KLM); two major airports

Communications	
Newspapers	75 dailies with a circulation of 4,700,000 (1990), including *De Telegraaf*, *De Volkskrant, De Krant op Zondag*
TV/Radio	Three national TV channels, Netherlands 1, 2, 3 Five national radio stations

Portugal (República Portuguesa)

Land area	92,082 sq. km
Capital	Lisbon
Currency	Escudo (Es) of 100 centavos
Languages	Portuguese
Religion	95% Roman Catholic (1990)
Head of State	President Mario Soares
Prime Minister	Anibal Cavaco Silva

Population Profile

Population (1990)	10,390,000
Active population (those in work or seeking work; 1988)	4,700,000

Population by age and sex (1989)

Age group	Total '000	%	Males '000	%	Females '000	%
0–4	636	6.3	328	3.2	308	3.0
5–9	738	7.4	380	3.7	358	3.5
10–14	843	8.4	431	4.2	412	4.0
15–24	1,726	17.2	877	8.5	849	8.2
25–34	1,555	15.5	777	7.5	778	7.5
35–44	1,270	12.7	615	6.0	655	6.4
45–54	1,122	11.2	529	5.1	593	5.8
55–64	1,089	10.9	500	4.9	589	5.7
65+	1,326	13.2	542	5.3	784	7.6
Total	10,305	100.0	4,978	48.4	5,327	51.7

Population per sq. km (1989)	112

Economic Profile

GNP per capita, US$ (1990)	4,260

Five biggest companies (1988)

Rank	Company	Sales Esc m	No. of employees
1	Petroleos de Portugal	338,000	5,970
2	Electricidade de Portugal	242,000	23,000
3	TAP (Transportes Aereos Portugueses)	112,401	23,000
4	Renault Portuguesa	97,941	3,582
5	Correios e Telecomunicaçoes	97,724	28,745

Sources: TEAM/Y&R.

Value of exports FOB, US$ bn (1989)	13.1
Value of imports CIF, US$ bn (1989)	18.5
Central bank	Banco de Portugal

Political Profile	
Constitution/ electoral system	Republic Assembly of the Republic has 230 deputies, elected every four years by universal suffrage at age 18
Local government	18 districts, consisting of 305 municipal authorities and 4,209 parishes. Assemblies are directly elected at each level The Azores and Madeira are autonomous regions, also with directly elected assemblies
Last election	October 1991
Results	Social Democrats (PSD) 135 Socialist Party (PS) 72 Communist Alliance 17 Christian Democrats 5 National Solidarity 1

International Relations	
Portugal is a member of	UN, EC, NATO, OECD, WEU, Council of Europe

Transport Infrastructure	
Rail	3,588 km of railways in 1989
Road	9,330 km of roads (1989)
	3,098,691 cars and trucks registered (1989)
Air	Main airline: Air Portugal; one major airport

Communications	
Newspapers	38 dailies including *Correio da Manhã, O Independente*
TV/Radio	Radio Difusão Portuguesa
	Radiotelevisão Portuguesa
	Radio Renancenca

Spain (Reino de España)

Land area	504,782 sq. km
Capital	Madrid
Currency	Peseta (Pta)
Languages	Spanish and Castilian are the official languages; there are many regional languages
Religion	99% Roman Catholic
Head of State	King Juan Carlos I
Prime Minister	Felipe González Márquez

Population Profile

Population (1989)	38,420,000
Active population (those in work or seeking work; 1989)	14,841,000

Population by age and sex (1986)

Age group	Total '000	%	Males '000	%	Females '000	%
0–4	2,294	6.0	1,179	3.1	1,114	2.9
5–9	3,061	8.0	1,573	4.1	1,488	3.9
10–14	3,289	8.5	1,687	4.4	1,602	4.2
15–24	6,485	16.9	3,307	8.6	3,178	8.3
25–34	5,465	14.2	2,753	7.2	2,712	7.0
35–44	4,688	12.2	2,345	6.1	2,344	6.1
45–54	4,339	11.3	2,135	5.5	2,204	5.7
55–64	4,163	10.8	1,998	5.2	2,165	5.6
65+	4,689	12.2	1,901	4.9	2,788	7.2
Total	38,473	100.0	18,878	49.1	19,595	50.9

Source: Institutuo Nacional de Estadistica.

Population per sq. km (1989)	74.7

Economic Profile

GNP per capita, US$ (1990)	12,610

Five biggest companies (1989)

Rank	Company	Sector	Sales Pta m	No. of employees
1	Repsol Petroleo	Petroleum	926,283	18,716
2	Telefonica de España	Public service	612,536	66,062
3	El Corte Ingles	Retail	475,283	33,953
4	E.N. de Electricidad	Electricity	457,502	15,678
5	Tabacalera	General/ Tobacco	443,443	8,701

Source: Magazine Mercado.

Value of exports FOB, US$ bn (1989)	45.4
Value of imports CIF, US$ bn (1989)	72.6
Central bank	Bank of Spain

Political Profile	
Constitution/ electoral system	Constitutional monarchy Congress of Deputies (lower house) has 350 members, elected every four years by universal adult suffrage at age 18 Senate (upper house) has 208 members, elected by the provinces
Local government	A semi-federal system of regional administration, with 17 autonomous communities each with an elected parliament and a regional government exercising legislative and executive powers in certain areas. Communities break down into 50 provinces made up of 8,066 municipalities. Each municipal council has an elected council and a mayor.
Last election	October 1989
Results	Socialists (PSOE) 175 Popular Party (PP) 107 Convergencia i Unio 18 United Left (IU) 17 Social and Democratic Centre (CDS) 14 Basque Nationalist (PNV) 5 Basque Separatist (HB) 4 Other regional parties 10

International Relations	
Spain is a member of	UN, EC, NATO, OECD, WEU, Council of Europe

Transport Infrastructure	
Rail	Red Nacional de Ferrovarriles Españoles (RENFE) 12,560 km
Road	2,344 km of motorway (1988) 10,788,975 cars registered
Air	Major airline: Iberia

Communications	
Newspapers	84 dailies (1989), daily circulation of 5 million copies, including *El Pais*, *Diario 16*, *ABC*, *La Vanguardia*
TV/Radio	Radio Nacional de España Sociedad Española de Radiodifusión (SER), Antena 3, Radio 8, Televisión Española Tele 5, Canal Plus

The United Kingdom

Land area	224,100 sq. km
Capital	London
Currency	Pound sterling (£) of 100 pence
Language	English
Religion	71% Protestant (established church is Church of England), 13% Roman Catholic, 16% others or unaffiliated
Head of State	Queen Elizabeth II
Prime Minister	John Major

Population Profile

Population (1989)	57,400,000
Active population (those in work or seeking work; 1990)	28,508,000

Population by age and sex (1989)

Age group	Total '000	Total %	Males '000	Males %	Females '000	Females %
0–4	3,671	6.6	1,881	3.4	1,791	3.2
5–9	3,500	6.3	1,794	3.2	1,705	3.1
10–14	3,259	5.9	1,675	3.0	1,584	2.8
15–24	8,457	15.2	4,315	7.8	4,141	7.4
25–34	8,359	15.0	4,215	7.6	4,144	7.4
35–44	7,680	13.8	3,845	6.9	3,835	6.9
45–54	6,232	11.2	3,115	5.6	3,117	5.6
55–64	5,726	10.3	2,783	5.0	2,942	5.3
65+	8,760	15.7	3,496	6.3	5,264	9.5
Total	55,643	100.0	27,119	48.8	28,524	51.2

Source: Office of Population, Censuses and Surveys, General Register Offices for Scotland and Northern Ireland.

Population per sq. km (1989)	228

Economic Profile

GNP per capita, US$ (1990)	14,570

Five biggest companies (1989)

Rank	Company	Sector	Market capital £ m	No. of employees
1	British Petroleum	Petroleum	15,747	125,950
2	British Telecom	Telecom-munications	15,120	242,723
3	Shell Transport/ Trading	Petroleum	13,757	—
4	Glaxo Holdings	Pharmaceutical	10,112	26,423
5	BAT Industries	General	9,877	310,779

Source: Financial Times Top 500.

Value of exports FOB, US$ bn (1989)	166
Value of imports CIF, US$ bn (1989)	215
Central bank	Bank of England

Political Profile	
Constitution/ electoral system	Constitutional monarchy House of Commons (lower house) has 651 members, elected every five years by universal suffrage at age 18 House of Lords (upper house) has 1,184 members, including hereditary peers and life peers appointed by the sovereign
Local government	Different systems exist for England and Wales, and for Scotland The six metropolitan counties are run by metropolitan district councils and exist alongside 47 non-metropolitan counties. County, district and parish councils are all directly elected and each elects a mayor. The counties consist of 369 districts and 10,000 parishes
Last election	April 1992
Results (seats in House of Commons)	Conservatives 336 Labour 271 Liberal Democrats 20 Ulster Unionists 9 Plaid Cymru 4 Social Democrat and Labour Party (N. Ireland) 3 Democratic Unionists 3 Ulster Popular Unionists 1

International Relations	
The United Kingdom is a member of	UN, EC, NATO, OECD, WEU, Council of Europe, Commonwealth, the Colombo Plan

Transport Infrastructure	
Rail	British Rail (BR) has approximately 17,702 km of track
Road	2,995 km of motorway (1989)
	24,196,000 vehicles registered
Air	Main airline: British Airways; six major airports

Communications	
Newspapers	13 national dailies (1992), including *The Times*, *Independent*, *Guardian*, *Daily Telegraph*, *Daily Mirror*, *Sun*
TV/Radio	Provided by the BBC (national public service broadcasting authority), IBA (national commercial authority) and independent contractors

2

Living and working in Europe

This chapter covers:
- The development and provisions of the Social Charter
- The difference between the Social Charter and the Social Chapter
- A summary of EC social policy in four areas: work, social protection, health and education
- A review of social provision in each of these four areas for each Community member state

Introduction

The opening up of Europe by the Single European Act of 1986, in particular with the coming into effect of the Single Market on 1 January 1993, has provided new opportunities for all its citizens to sample life in member states other than their own. It is now much easier not only to travel around Europe as a visitor, but also to live and work in other EC countries.

It is therefore important to be aware of the factors affecting life both within and outside the workplace in the various states – the more so because, as this chapter will show, these factors vary enormously from one country to another.

To enable comparisons between countries, the latter part of this chapter is divided, like chapter 1, into sections dealing with the individual states. Each section sets out the provisions in that country relating to:

- working conditions;
- social protection;
- health;
- education.

However, national provisions are only part of the story. The Community itself has since its inception taken a strong interest in the development of living and working conditions for all its citizens, and this – now commonly referred to as Community 'social policy' – has been and continues to be a prominent and controversial policy area.

Social Charter and Social Chapter

Central to Community policy on living and working conditions is the Community Charter of Fundamental Social Rights for Workers (the 'Social Charter'), signed by eleven of the twelve member states – not the UK – in December 1989. These principles were further enshrined in the Social Chaper of the Maastricht Treaty, which again met with strong resistance from Britain.

For details of the Social Chapter see chapter 8.

The Social Charter grew out of the conviction held by many of those in the policy-making circles of the Community that the protection of workers is vital to the economic progress and development of the EC. Not all Europe's workers were adequately protected already: of the 128 million strong European workforce, 8 million are self-employed; and 40 per cent of all employment is provided by small and medium-sized enterprises which often lack either the means or the will effectively to protect their own employees.

THE SOCIAL CHARTER

The fundamental rights covered in the Charter are as follows:

Freedom of movement
> Every worker in the EC is free to move about the EC, to take up any occupation or profession in an EC country, and to be treated in the same way as a national of that country in terms of access to employment, working conditions and social protection.

Employment and remuneration
> Every worker may work in whichever occupation field s/he chooses, providing s/he has the appropriate and relevant qualifications and satisfies any rules which govern that occupation. Each worker is also entitled to fair pay for that occupation.

Improvement of living and working conditions
> It is a continuing aim of the Community to develop legislation to ensure that each worker gets a fair deal in terms of paid annual leave, weekly rest periods, redundancy provision, etc. Conditions should be laid out in a worker's contract of employment.

continued . . .

Social protection

Every worker has the right to an adequate level of social protection with the appropriate social security benefits. This right also applies to those who are not in employment.

Freedom of association and collective bargaining

Workers are entitled to join trade unions and employers are free to form professional organizations to protect their own interests. Both workers and employers have the right not to join any organization. Collective agreements can be negotiated by unions and professional organizations in line with national legislation and practice. The right to strike is subject to any obligation laid down in national regulations and collective agreements.

Vocational training

Every worker should have access to vocational training during his/her working life.

Equal treatment for men and women

People of both sexes should be given equal opportunity and treatment in respect of employment, education and training.

Information, consultation and participation for workers

All organizations should have a system of information, consultation and participation for its workforce. This is particularly important where a company operates in more than one member state.

Health, protection and safety in the workplace

Every worker is entitled to satisfactory health and safety conditions in the workplace.

Protection of children and young people

The minimum age of employment should not be lower than 15 or the minimum school leaving age. Under-18s should not do any nightwork. Young people should receive a fair rate of pay and are entitled to initial vocational training.

Elderly people

Every retired worker should have a decent standard of living. Those without a pension should receive adequate resources as well as medical and social assistance.

Disabled people

The disabled are entitled to be integrated socially and professionally. They should enjoy adequate provision in transport, training and housing.

In February 1988 the Commission published a paper on the development of the Community's social policy, highlighting the need for intensified dialogue between social partners on social policy issues. This came to be commonly known as the 'social dialogue'.

The most prominent advocate of a strengthened common social policy has been the President of the Commission, Jacques Delors. He has contended that the Single Market brought into being by the Single European Act should benefit individuals living and working in the EC as much as business organizations: that is, that the Act should set in motion social as well as economic reform. He declared that the Act should contain a 'social dimension' which would cover the whole area of social policy and the free movement of labour:

The social dimension permeates all our discussions and everything we do: our efforts to restore competitiveness and cooperate on macroeconomic policy to reduce unemployment and provide all young Europeans with a working future; common policies designed to promote the development of less-prosperous regions and the regeneration of regions hit by industrial change; employment policy and the concentration of efforts on helping young people to gain a foothold in the labour market and combating long-term unemployment; and the development of rural regions threatened by the decline in the number of farms, desertification and demographic imbalances.

Think what a boost it would be for democracy and social injustice if we could demonstrate that we are capable of working together to create a better integrated society open to all.

Three controversial issues need to be cleared up in this context.

First, the Charter of social rights. Its sole object is to provide a formal reminder that the Community has no intention of sacrificing fundamental workers' rights on the altar of economic efficiency. How could anyone object to such an idea, which is to be found in all our social traditions? How could anyone dispute the political and rhetorical significance of this message for a people's Europe, for the man in the street? When it comes to translating these principles into legislation or collective bargaining subsidiarity comes into its own, ensuring that our different traditions are respected. This is borne out by the Commission's social programme, which will be implemented within the bounds of the Treaty as it now stands.

Jacques Delors
Bruges, 17 October 1989

Britain and the Social Charter

The reluctance of the British government to adopt the Social Charter and Social Chapter stems from its belief that British industry must be self-directing, allowed to operate free from undue interference from national or supranational authority. It further contends that in order to maintain competitiveness, British industry must retain total autonomy, and therefore flexibility, in setting its wage rates and working hours.

Many other member states, in contrast to Britain, already have national legislation in place which meets or even exceeds the Charter's requirements.

Controversy in this area will inevitably continue during the 1990s, as pressures for a common level of social protection throughout Europe mount on the one hand, and the economic environment becomes ever more competitive on the other.

Social Policy in Europe: A Review

Before turning to a country-by-country analysis of work and social provision, it is worthwhile briefly reviewing the state of affairs across the EC as a whole in the four main areas addressed in this chapter: work, social protection, health and education.

Work

Levels of employment and working conditions vary considerably across the EC. Despite moves to harmonize working conditions through the Social Charter (see above) and the Social Chapter of the Maastricht Treaty (see chapter 8), there remain differences that are different to eliminate, particularly in view of the different rates at which member states' economies are developing. Working conditions also vary according to national custom and practice, cultural conditions and attitudes towards work, and political objectives.

Understandably during a period of world recession in the early 1990s, unemployment is a major concern for most European countries. In 1989 there were 12.7 million unemployed in the Community (9% of the active population).

Social Protection

The degree of commitment to social protection and the benefits provided to citizens vary widely among the member states (see figure 2.1.)

Pensions account for the largest proportion of social protection expenditure in the EC as a whole (45% in 1987), followed by health care (36% in 1987).

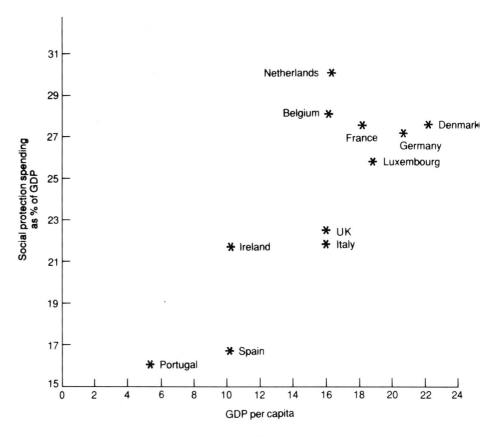

Figure 2.1 Percentage of GDP devoted to social protection, and per capita GDP, in member states in 1988 (for Belgium, Spain and UK: 1987)
Source: *Eurostat*

Expenditure on social protection tends to be raised from three main sources: contributions from employers; contributions from employees; and public funds. Each country applies a unique blend of these sources. For example, in 1987 Denmark raised 77.9% of contributions from public funds, 10.9% from employers, 4.3% from employees and 6.8% from other receipts; in the same period the Netherlands raised 14.2% from public funds, 33.2% from employers, 35.6% from employees and 16.8% from other receipts (in this case, interest on invested capital).

Health

The Community's citizens by and large enjoy good health supported by well-developed health services. Subject to neither extremes of climate nor extremes of general poverty, Europe escapes many of the severe health problems suffered in harsher and poorer regions of the world. There are, however, areas of concern that all twelve member states have to confront, although their methods and structures of health provision vary widely.

Statistics published by the World Health Organization highlight the following areas:

- Diseases of the circulatory system and malignant tumours are the major causes of death in the EC, accounting for 45% and 24% of deaths respectively.
- Aids is a matter for increasing concern: at 1 January 1990 there were 22,940 registered cases in the EC among men between the ages of 20 and 54.
- Road accidents accounted for 45,000 deaths and 1,604,831 cases of injury in 1987. Almost three-quarters of those killed were male, and almost half of these were aged between 15 and 34.

Education

The last two decades have seen a number of trends emerge in education within the Community. The number of pupils and students in the EC as a whole increased by 7% although this was not consistent over all levels. In 1986/7 72% of Europeans aged between 5 and 24 were in full-time education, with the equivalent figure in France reaching 82.8%. The biggest increase was within the tertiary sector (further and higher education), due primarily to an increase in the number of female students. Numbers of pupils in secondary education also rose; but the greatest movement came in the fall in the numbers of primary school pupils, due to the declining birthrate in Europe.

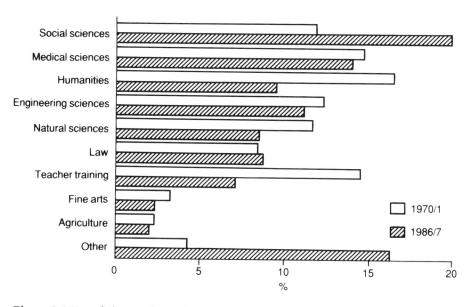

Figure 2.2 Trends in numbers of students in various subject fields at tertiary level in all 12 member states
Source: Eurostat

For tertiary education, subject choice has also changed over the years: see figure 2.2.

Computer literacy is spreading throughout Europe's youth: 47% of young people in the EC now claim to be able to use a computer, although the figures show marked disparities among member states, with just 19% of Greeks and Portuguese claiming to be computer literate compared to 69% of Danes, Britons and Luxembourgeois.

Belgium

Working life: the national provisions

Working week
    Maximum 40 hours; usual 38–9 hours
    No Sunday working

Public holidays
    11 days

Paid holidays
    20 days minimum after one year's service; usually 24 days.
    Salaried employees receive paid salary plus 85% bonus

Minimum wage
    Minimum wage for 150 sectors.
    Other sectors: BFr 39, 156 ($1,175) per month. All employees
    have pay raised automatically twice a year

Sick pay
    Employees get one month's salary; manual workers get
    seven days'. Rest of year at 60% of earnings

Maternity leave
    15 weeks at 79.5% of earnings up to BFr 3, 033 ($90) a day,
    plus BFr 31, 289 ($940) grant for first child and BFr 21, 580 for
    each thereafter

Termination
    Three months' notice for each commenced five-year period
    of service for employees; for manual workers, minimum 28
    days' notice

Works council
    Over 50 employees: firm must have health and safety
    council; over 100 employees, must have works council

Social protection

- Social security contributions are made to a central department called the National Social Security Office.
- Contributions are paid in part by the employee and in part by the employer; the state provides any remaining amount.
- Every active citizen is obliged by law to contribute to the social security system.
- Social security forms a major part of government expenditure.
- Other organizations which focus on social protection issues are the Centre Public d'Aide Sociale for French-speaking parts of the country and the Openbaar Centrum voor Maatschappelijk Welzijn for Flemish-speaking areas. These agencies work through the local system of communes.
- In 1989 the yearly average for social protection benefits per head was 3,517 Ecu.
- The major benefits are:
  - sickness and invalidity;
  - insurance;
  - old age and survivors' pensions;
  - unemployment benefit;
  - child benefit.

Health

- Belgium's health care system gives a high standard of care to its citizens.
- Doctors' and dentists' fees and charges are largely reimbursed by social insurance.
- Health care expenditure accounts for more than 7% of the gross national product; this proportion has more than doubled over the past 30 years.
- There is one doctor and one dentist to every 300 inhabitants.
- Life expectancy is 78 for women and 71 for men.
- Provision for 1989/90 indicates 33,000 doctors, 7,300 dentists and 50,354 hospital beds.

Education

- Education is free and compulsory for children from 6 to 18 years.
- Compulsory education is the responsibility of the Flemish and Walloon communities.
- The education system is currently undergoing change following the constitutional reform of 1988.
- *Pre-school:* voluntary kindergartens and nurseries are available but attendance is not compulsory.

- *Primary:* primary and infant schools number around 9,000.
- *Secondary:* there are 2,000 middle schools which offer both general and technical classes.
- *Tertiary:* there are seven state and 10 private universities; student numbers total just over 100,000.

Denmark

Working life: the national provisions

Working week
> 37 hours maximum. Regular overtime against national collective agreement.

Public holidays
> 12 days

Paid holidays
> 30 days minimum. Salaried employees get normal wage plus holiday bonus of 1% of previous year's total salary

Minimum wages
> National collective agreement governing dismissals, wages, etc. agreed between main employers and employees' organization

Sick pay
> Salaried employees get full pay during sick leave. Non-salaried employees entitled to two weeks; rest from state.

Maternity leave
> 28 weeks. Four weeks' leave before birth, paid by social security. After birth, both parents entitled to total of 24 weeks' leave at DKr, 2,457 ($390) a week

Termination
> Minimum of one month's salary only after 12 years' service; two months' after 15 years; three months' after 18 years

Works council
> Every company with 35 or more employees must have cooperation committees

Social protection

- Denmark is proud of its claim to be a welfare state and one third of its expenditure goes on social services. The statement can be justified in part at least by highlighting the high degree of income

redistribution stemming from a fairly punitive tax system.
- Denmark has the highest level of social protection benefits per head in the EC at a yearly average of 5,334 Ecu.
- The social protection system provides free medical care and sickness allowance, pensions, unemployment benefit, family allowances, etc.
- Everyone over the age of 67 is entitled to a state old-age pension which is exempt from tax. Supplementary pensions are available for anyone who has only the old-age pension and a limited income.
- Denmark also gives paternity leave: a father is entitled to two weeks' leave after the birth.
- Family allowance is granted to all children under the age of 18 regardless of family income.

Health

- The Danes had the highest rate of household expenditure on alcohol and tobacco of any country in the Community in 1987; however, their health as reflected in the statistics is relatively good.
- Life expectancy is 77 for women and 71 for men.
- In 1986 Denmark had 2.6 doctors per 1,000 inhabitants and 11 hospital beds per 1,000 inhabitants.
- The only area where Denmark performs poorly against its EC neighbours are suicide, where the Danes have the highest rate for both men and women, and Aids, where they have the third highest rate.

Education

- Schooling between ages 7 and 16 is free and compulsory.

Pre-school

- In 1989 69.6% of Danish 3–6 year-olds attended kindergartens or pre-school classes (børnehaveklasse).

Primary

- 91% of all Danish children attend primary school, called 'Folkeskole' (people's school).
- Starting at age 7, the Folkeskole lasts for nine years; an optional tenth year may be added.
- In practice streaming does not often occur in the compulsory nine year period although there may be some in the eighth and ninth forms.
- At the end of nine or ten years pupils can sit an exam, which is however not compulsory, in order to receive a final grade.

Secondary

- Two-thirds of Folkeskole pupils go on to some form of vocational or practical training; one-third goes on to secondary schools, of which there are three distinct kinds.
- At the 'gymnasium' (upper secondary school), students take a specialist route, focusing on, e.g., maths or languages; they study for three years and take final exams.
- Alternatively, students can take a two-year course with a final exam at the 'studenterkursus' (adult upper secondary school), or a two-year higher preparatory examination course with a final exam, which prepares pupils for university or other higher-education.
- Vocational education and training includes apprenticeship training and covers courses in many occupational fields, e.g. commerce and trade, construction, graphics, service trades, food, agriculture, transport and communication, amongst others.

Tertiary

- Tertiary education in Denmark comprises all education following the twelfth year of education and is divided into short courses of further education and long courses of higher education.
- There are five universities in Denmark.
- There are also institutions of higher education for engineering, pharmacy, dentistry, architecture and many other professions.

France

Working life: the national provisions

Working week
> Normal week defined as 39 hours; eight hours a day maximum for apprentices and young workers, 10 for adults

Public holidays
> 11 (13 in Alsace–Lorraine). Usually extra day off when holiday on Tuesday or Thursday

Paid holidays
> 30 days a year minimum, to be taken between 1 May and 31 October. Four days' paid leave for marriage

Minimum wage
> Salaire Minimum Interprofessionel de Croissance sets minimum FFr 5,520 ($990) a month. Revised each July. Collective agreements cover all sectors

continued . . .

Sick pay
> National insurance scheme provides minimum pay for all sick workers based on basic salary

Maternity leave
> 16 or 24 weeks. Family with one or two children: six weeks before birth, 10 after; family with three or more children, eight weeks before, 18 after. Benefit is 84% of salary, tax-free

Termination
> Minimum one month's notice for six months' to two years' service; two months for over two years

Works council
> Every company with 50 or more employees must have works council; with 100 or more, must start profit-sharing scheme

---

Social protection

- France has a comprehensive policy covering social security. Social protection benefits per head are fairly high at an average of 4,107 Ecu per year.
- The general scheme, which covers two-thirds of the population, is an insurance scheme funded by contributions from both employees and employers, as well as the state. It covers sickness, maternity, death, invalidity, old age, accidents at work and family benefits, paid only to those who can prove a certain level of contributions.
- There is also a separate, autonomous unemployment benefit scheme.
- The insurance scheme is supplemented by an assistance scheme managed by local authorities. It is made up generally of non-contributary benefits which also cover such areas as old-age pensions.

Health

- Health care in France is provided by a mixture of public and private organizations: the sickness insurance system, the social aid scheme for those without social security cover, or via the private sector.
- Medical care provided by GPs is paid for by the patient who is reimbursed later. Reimbursement will typically cover around 75% of the charge the patient paid.
- The cost of hospital treatment is paid directly by the state.
- In 1988 there were 596,476 hospital beds and 144,071 doctors in France.
- French women have the highest life expectancy of all the member states at 80.6 years; for men the figure is 72.6 years.

- France has the worst record in the EC for Aids cases, reporting 158.3 cases per million inhabitants in January 1990.

Education

- Education is compulsory between the ages of 6 and 16.
- Education is free at all state schools (four-fifths of all schools).

Pre-school

- Classes for children aged 2–5 are often given as infant classes attached to primary schools.
- Priority is given to children from socially underprivileged backgrounds.

Primary

- This covers ages 6–11 and comprises three stages: preparatory (one year), elementary (two years) and intermediary (two years).
- Pupils study three groups of subjects: French, history, geography and civics; mathematics, science and technology; and physical education and sport, art and craft work and music.

Secondary

- At age 11 all school children move on to either a college or a lycée.
- The college will be either a Collège d'Enseignement General (CEG), or a Collège d'Enseignement Technique (CET). Both educate pupils up to age 18.
- Education between the ages of 11 and 15 is split into two cycles: the observation stage (cycle d'observation) and the orientation stage (cycle d'orientation).
- Some pupils will enter a lycée instead of a CEG or CET. The lycées provide an education which will prepare the pupil for either the general or technical baccalauréat examination, taken in the final year.
- There are also lycées professionnels, vocational lycées, offering courses which lead to vocational certificates, e.g. the Brevet d'enseignement professionnel, the Certificat d'aptitude professionnelle, and the Baccalauréat professionnel.

Tertiary

- There are 69 universities and three national polytechnic institutes as well as a number of private and Catholic universities.
- Higher education is also available in over 400 schools and institutes including the 177 Grandes Ecoles. These world-famous centres of excellence are selective institutions offering technological and commercial curricula. They have been responsible for producing many members of the elite who govern France.

Germany

Working life: the national provisions

Working week
> 48 hours maximum; most staff contracted to work five-day
> week of 37–40 hours in west, 40–44 in east

Public holidays
> 10 (14 in Catholic areas). Usually extra day off when holiday
> on Thursday

Paid holidays
> Three weeks minimum; usually 28–31 days in west and 21–26
> days in east. In west, extra month's salary usually paid as
> holiday bonus

Minimum wage
> Terms of collective agreements on areas like contracts,
> salaries and hours are legally binding for nearly all
> employees

Sick pay
> Employers pay sick pay for six weeks; local sickness funds
> provide for time after this

Maternity leave
> 14 to 18 weeks at normal salary. Either parent can take leave
> up to 18 months after birth. State pays DM 600 ($370)
> monthly allowance for 18 months

Termination
> Notice can only be given six weeks before end of each
> quarter year. For salaried staff minimum compensation is six
> weeks' pay

Works council
> Every company with five or more employees must have an
> elected works council

Social protection

- Germany was one of the first countries in Europe to devise social
  protection schemes for its citizens and appropriately has a
  comprehensive system of protection today.
- Nearly 30% of the gross national product in Germany goes on
  providing social benefits and services. Social protection benefits per
  head are generous at an average of 4,594 Ecu per year.

- The Social Health Insurance scheme offers the following benefits: medical treatment, medicines, hospital care, maternity benefit, sickness payments, accident insurance and social assistance. Old-age pensions are available to wage earners and salaried employers as well as some of the self-employed. Family allowance and unemployment benefit are also available.

Health

- In 1990 there were over 238,000 doctors in Germany and around 830,000 hospital beds.
- Whilst excellent on a national scale, health care provision is not distributed evenly, however; some rural areas in particular are not as well provided for as others. This is considered to be a short-term problem which will soon be overcome.
- Life expectancy in 1992 was 78 years for women and 72 for men.

Education

- Education is compulsory for children aged 6–15 full time and for young people aged 16–18 part time.

Pre-school

- Kindergartens are not part of the state school system, and fees are charged for attendance. Nevertheless they are very popular: over 80% of all 3–6-year-olds in Germany attend kindergartens.

Primary

- Attendance is for four to six years at the Grundschule, up to age 10 or 11.

Secondary

- Junior secondary schools are called Hauptschule; around one-third of primary school children go on to this type of school for five years. Then, at the age of 15 or 16 the child can go on to take a course of vocational training until the age of 18.
- Intermediate schools (Realschule) have a six-year course of study which leads to a graduating certificate. This certificate allows pupils to attend a technical school (Fachschule), which offers vocational training at an upper secondary level. About one-third of all pupils gain the intermediate certificate.
- The Gymnasium's period of study lasts for nine years. This is the traditional grammar school equivalent and leads to the maturity certificate or 'Abitur', which is vital for university entrance.

Vocational education

- This is a key strength of Germany's education system.
- Over 90% of pupils who terminate their full-time education following completion of the junior secondary or intermediate stage go into vocational training.
- Vocational training is the compulsory for anyone attending no other type of school up to the age of 18.
- Commonly called the dual system, this is a joint initiative between the government, the state governments and private enterprise and state which gives both on-the-job experience and instruction in vocational schools.

Higher education

- German universities are older than most other European universities and generally their courses last longer than most. On average a student will spend seven years at university completing a degree.
- There are around 60 institutions of university status with almost 1.7 million students attending them.

Greece

Working life: the national provisions

Working week
>   Standard week is 40 hours. Mix of five-day and six-day week; unusual for Saturday to be day off, except in civil service

Public holidays
>   12 days

Paid holidays
>   Four weeks' minimum after one year's service. All employees must be paid annual bonus equal to two months' salary. Six days off for marriage

Minimum wage
>   General Collective Labour Agreement (GCLA) sets minimum monthly wage of Dr 78,272 ($390). Other agreements must match GLCA

Sick pay
>   Salaried employees: first three days at half pay. Full salary for one month after one year's service *continued...*

Maternity leave
> 15 weeks (105 days): 52 days before birth and 53 after.
> Mother entitled to one hour's paid leave during work to feed
> and care for child for first year after birth

Termination
> One month's notice after two months' service for salaried
> employees; up to six months after 10 years. Minimum
> compensation is half minimum notice

Works council
> Every company with 50 or more employees (20 or more if no
> recognized trade union) must have a works council

Social protection

- In 1988 social protection benefits per capita were one of the lowest in the EC at just 658 Ecu per year.
- There is a system of sick pay for salaried employees as well as provision for maternity leave.
- Old-age pensions are financed by insurance schemes; occupational schemes are unusual.

Health

- Greece has over 50,000 hospital beds and more than 32,000 doctors for its population.
- Life expectancy for women is 77.6 years and for men 72.6 years.

Education

- The education system is free and starts at the age of 6.
- Primary education is compulsory.
- In 1987–8 there were over 5,000 kindergartens, more than 8,000 primary schools and almost 3,000 high schools and lycea.
- There are 13 universities in Greece.

Ireland

Working life: the national provisions

Working week
> Maximum 48 hours a week, nine hours a day. No working after 8 p.m. Usual week 39 hours

Public holidays
> Eight days

Paid holidays
> Three weeks minimum for most employees in private sector after eight months' service. Employer decides when holiday is taken

Minimum wage
> No statutory minimum. In 14 industries where union representation is weak (e.g. agriculture, catering) Joint Labour Committee sets minimum rates

Sick pay
> After three days, Ir£48 ($78) a week for 18 days, then plus 12% of earnings for one year

Maternity leave
> 14 weeks, of which four weeks must be taken before birth and four after. Maternity benefit is 70% of gross earnings; minimum Ir£76 ($125) a week, maximum Ir£154 ($250) a week

Termination
> Compensation for at least two years' service is half a week's pay for every year served, rising to a week a year when aged over 41

Works council
> No legal requirement for companies to have works councils

Social protection

- Average social protection benefits per head in 1988 came to 1,719 Ecu.
- Social insurance is compulsory for all employees and the self-employed, and is also contributed to by employers and the state.
- There is also a system of social aid with benefits to help people who fall outside the scheme. Typical benefits covered are child benefit, family income supplement and assistance for the elderly.

- Social insurance benefits include (among others) old-age pensions, widows' pensions, disability benefit, invalidity payments, unemployment benefit and maternity benefit.
- The Department of Social Welfare also provides a range of benefits in kind mainly for the elderly and disabled. These include free travel, free electricity allowance, free gas allowance, free telephone rental, free TV licence, and fuel allowance.

Health

- The Department of Health, under the control of the Minister for Health, is responsible for the health service in Ireland, with regional health boards controlling services at local level.
- Health care is not entirely free. Lower income groups (around 37% of the population) receive medical services free of charge; for the remainder of the population public hospital services and visits to the family doctor are available for a minimal charge. There is a system of voluntary health insurance to help meet the cost of medical treatment.
- Ireland is the only country in the EC with a birth rate high enough to be replacing its population; despite this, the birth rate is still falling quite rapidly.
- Life expectancy is 76.7 years for women and 71 years for men.

Education

- In 1990 more than 25% of the country's total population was in full-time education (968,684 people).
- Education is free and compulsory between the ages of 6 and 15.

Primary

- Primary education in Ireland is state-aided, but run by local Committees of Management.

Secondary

- This level of education covers pupils of age 12 and upwards.
- Some schools are state-owned, others are state-aided. Many secondary schools are run by religious orders.
- Once secondary schooling is completed, pupils may sit the Leaving Certificate examination.
- There are 16 comprehensive schools which are financed by the state. These schools combine academic and technical subjects. Pupils take state exams and may go on to enter institutes of further education or universities.

- Vocational Education Committee Schools provide general and technical education. They are sometimes amalgamated with voluntary secondary schools to form Community schools.

Tertiary

- Ireland has four universities, the most famous of which is Trinity College, Dublin University.
- There are also regional technical colleges and colleges of technology throughout the country. These institutions focus on applied science and technological education.

Italy

Working life: the national provisions

Working week
> Maximum 48 hours a week, eight hours a day; usual week 40 hours

Public holidays
> 10, plus two public holidays held on Sundays for which there is payment in lieu

Paid holidays
> 23 days average. Minimum levels set out in various national collective agreements. Fifteen days off for marriage

Minimum wage
> Minimum pay in 200 national collective labour contracts set with reference to job, seniority (up to director level) and cost of living. Revised annually

Sick pay
> All employers covered by national plan. Sick pay covered by plan, or employer, or both, funding most or all of salary

Maternity leave
> 22 weeks or more. Benefit (taxable) of 80% of gross salary. Optional six months with taxable benefit of 30% of gross salary. Parents may work two hours less a day for one year

Termination
> Employees get compensation of 7.4% of actual gross salary earned for each year in service, adjusted for inflation

Works council
> Every company with 15 or more employees must have a works council

Social protection

- Social protection provision covers pensions, family allowances and health services. Pensions are linked to a price index.
- Benefits are paid to families from central government and social security departments.
- In 1989 average social protection benefits per head came to 3,025 Ecu.

Health

- Italian health services are administered by the Unità Sanitaria Locale and are therefore a regional responsibility, although funded by central government.
- Medical consultations are free, but since April 1989 patients have had to pay a proportion of prescription costs.
- In 1986 and 1988 there were approximately 245,000 doctors and 424,000 hospital beds respectively.
- Life expectancy is 79.1 years for women and 72.6 for men.

Education

Pre-school

- There are two levels of provision for pre-school education, neither of which is compulsory: day nursery ('nidi d'infanzia') and nursery school proper.
- Day nurseries are for children under 3 and are often privately run.
- Nursery schools are for children aged 3–5 and may be either private ventures or run by religious or local groups.
- The general aim of nursery education is to prepare pupils for entry into the compulsory system.

Primary

- Primary education is provided by both public and private institutions. The public sector is free and education in both sectors is compulsory between the ages of 6 and 14.
- There is a national curriculum system and formal testing takes place at the end of the five–year period at age 11.
- Each pupil has a 'scheda' (personal record card) which gives a profile of his or her personality.
- The primary school certificate allows progress to secondary education.

Secondary

- This may last for three, four or five years according to the route taken.
- A pupil may complete his/her compulsory education at the scuola media (lower-secondary school) after three years, when a final exam is taken based on a compulsory curriculum. Successful students are awarded a Diploma di Licenza Media.
- Courses at the higher secondary school (Liceo) last four or five years and students are admitted on successful completion of the scuola media. The curriculum is compulsory. At the end of a course successful candidates are awarded a Diploma di Maturitá.
- Students with a five-year diploma can proceed to university automatically; holders of the four-year diploma must first take a special one-year preparatory course.
- Higher secondary education is subdivided into classical, scientific and language schools, professional institutes and technical education.

Tertiary

- Universities are state-run and courses can be of four, five or six years' duration.
- A degree course is called 'Corso di Laurea'. There are also the 'Diploma Universitario' and 'Laurea breve', which are first-line degrees issued after two or three years of study.

Luxembourg

Working life: the national provisions

Working week
    Maximum 48 hours a week, 10 hours a day. Usually 39 or 40 hours a week

Public holidays
    12 days

Paid holidays
    25 days minimum after three months' service

Minimum wage
    Minimum wage set twice yearly. For unskilled worker with no family: LuxFr 36,819 ($1,100) a month. National collective agreements cover most workers

Sick pay
    Statutory sick pay paid for up to 52 weeks at basic salary

continued . . .

Maternity leave
> 16 weeks, eight weeks before birth and eight weeks after, plus additional four weeks if mother is breast-feeding. Qualification: six months' social security contributions in year before birth

Termination
> Two months' compensation for service up to five years; four months for five to 10 years; six months for over 10 years

Works council
> Every company with 15 or more employees must have a representative council; with 150 or more, must have a works council

Social protection

- Luxembourg has a fairly comprehensive social protection scheme which covers old-age pensions, maternity leave and sick pay, among other benefits.
- Social protection benefits per head are among the highest in the EC at 4,166 Ecu per year on average.

Health

- For a relatively affluent nation, the life expectancy in Luxembourg is lower than one might expect at 77.9 years for women and 70.6 for men. This is one of the lowest figures in the EC.
- The health service in Luxembourg provides 9.7 hospital beds per 1,000 habitants (the highest figure in the EC), but only 1.8 doctors per 1000 inhabitants which ranks in front of only the UK and Ireland.

Education

- Education is compulsory between the ages of 6 and 15.
- Inevitably for such a small state, the number of educational institutions is small.
- In 1988/9 there were approximately 8,000 pupils attending nursery schools, 26,000 at primary schools, 14,000 at technical secondary schools and 8,000 at secondary schools.
- In higher education students chose between university studies, teacher training and studies at the Higher Institute of Technology.

The Netherlands

Working life: the national provisions

Working week
>   Maximum 40 hours a week, eight hours a day. Weekend
>   working generally prohibited. Usual week 36 or 38 hours

Public holidays
>   Nine days

Paid holidays
>   Four weeks minimum after one year's service. Frequently
>   increased to five weeks. Two days off for marriage

Minimum wage
>   Minimum monthly wage of Fl 2,102 ($1,140), reviewed every
>   six months, for all workers 23 years and over

Sick pay
>   All entitled to paid sick leave after two days, at 70% of
>   earnings, for one year

Maternity leave
>   16 weeks (20 under some collective agreements), four weeks
>   of which must be taken before birth. Mothers and fathers
>   with one year's service with children under 4 may work
>   shorter hours for six months

Termination
>   Minimum notice for salaried employees one month; one
>   week for weekly paid workers; plus one week for every
>   year worked, up to 13 weeks

Works council
>   Every company with 35 or more employees must have works
>   council which meets with management at least six times a
>   year

Social protection

- The Dutch enjoy a comprehensive system of social security provision.
- In 1989 the average social protection benefits per head came to 3,949 Ecu per year.
- Under the Health Insurance Act anyone with an annual earned income of less than Fl 50,900 (1990) pays a monthly contribution and is then entitled to receive medical, pharmaceutical, dental and

hospital treatment. People earning over this amount must take out private medical insurance.

- Other benefits available are family allowance, old-age pensions, sickness benefit and unemployment benefit. There is also provision made in case of disablement, for widows and orphans and for national assistance.

Health

- The Netherlands enjoys a high standard of health care. The government's objective, as stated by the Ministry of Foreign Affairs, is 'to create a statutory framework and facilities to prevent disease and accidents and to promote the treatment, nursing and care of those who need it'.
- Life expectancy is around 79 years for women and 72 for men.
- Health care is financed mainly through an insurance system.
- The state does provide some funds, for example it funds the Municipal Health Services. It is also active in preventative medicine, funding vaccination programmes for children and school dental services, medical research and the training of health workers.
- Most health-care facilities are provided by non-governmental and private organizations, many of which began as charities. They are subject to state approval.
- In 1991 there were around 38,000 doctors and 65,000 licensed hospital beds.

Education

- Education is compulsory between the ages of 5 and 16.
- Compulsory education is generally free, though some schools will ask for a financial contribution from parents.
- Freedom of education is guaranteed by the constitution and private and state schools receive equal funding from government.
- Approximately 75% of all existing Dutch schools were set up by private bodies and associations.
- Four million of the population are in full-time education.

Pre-school

- Play groups and creches exist, but are not part of the state system and do not come under the control of the Ministry of Education and Science.

Primary

- Primary education covers children aged 4–12; school attendance becomes compulsory from the age of 5.

- The first two years concentrate on the skills of reading, writing, arithmetic and manual skills.
- From the age of 6 to 12 the curriculum concentrates on Dutch, maths, writing, history, geography, science and social studies. In the final year at primary school pupils learn English.

Secondary

- There are three types of secondary school: general secondary school; pre-university school; and vocational secondary school
- Junior and senior general schools offer four- and five-year courses respectively.
- Pre-university schools (called atheneum or gymnasium) offer six-year courses in preparation for higher or university education.
- Vocational education can be followed at junior, senior or higher level.
- Pupils on all of the secondary school courses are required to take written state examinations. The number of subjects taken and the level of the exams vary.
- Pupils who leave full-time education at the age of 16 are required by law to attend courses of continued training or education for one or two days a week.

Tertiary

- Higher education includes higher vocational courses at colleges and university education. There are eight universities and five 'hogescholen', which also provide university-level education.
- All universities are financed by government funds, irrespective of whether they are state or private foundations.
- University courses are split into two phases. The first phase takes four years and concludes with the 'doctoraal' examination. A limited number of students is admitted to the second phase where the student undertakes specialized study or research leading to a doctorate.

Portugal

Working life: the national provisions

Working week
Maximum 45 hours a week. In practice, 40–45 hours for industrial workers, 38 hours for clerks, 40–44 for shop workers

Public holidays
12 days

Paid holidays
30 days minimum after one year's service. Employees are entitled to two additional holiday bonuses of one month's salary

Minimum wage
Annual minimum for all full- and part-time employees: Es 40,100 ($280) a month for industry, services and agriculture; Es 33,500 ($235) for domestic service

Sick pay
After three days, statutory sick pay is 65% of normal wages for three years. Usually made up by employer

Maternity leave
13 weeks (90 days), of which 60 must be taken after birth. Maternity benefit is normal salary. Employee entitled to two 30-minute reductions in working hours daily for breast-feeding

Termination
Minimum notice for salaried workers is 15 days per year of service up to 15 years and one month a year thereafter

Works council
All companies must have works councils which meet with management at least once a month

Social protection

- The system of benefits in Portugal is financed partly by employees' and employers' contributions and partly by the state.
- There is a general scheme, membership in which is compulsory for the employed and self-employed, and also a non-contributory scheme which protects those who are not covered by the general scheme and who are in need.

- The scheme provides protection against unemployment, disability, old age, death, sickness, maternity and work injuries. It also provides family benefits.
- In 1988 average social protection benefits per head were 545 Ecu: the lowest figure in the EC, significantly behind all the other member states apart from Greece.

Health

- Perhaps not surprisingly for one of the poorer countries in the EC, life expectancy is towards the lower end of the range at 77.7 years for women and 70.6 years for men.
- Portugal has the lowest number of hospital beds per 1,000 inhabitants of the EC countries at just 2.9 (the highest is Luxembourg with 9.7).
- In 1989 there were around 28,000 doctors in Portugal.

Education

- Education is compulsory between the ages of 6 and 14.
- Pre-school classes cater for 3–6 years-olds. There is free nursery school provision in the public sector.
- Primary schools cater for children aged 6–10; from here pupils move into preparatory education, which covers 10–12-year-olds.
- Secondary education covers a period of six years but is not compulsory beyond age 14. Pupils aged 12–14 follow a general course before they are streamed into specialist areas at the age of 15 or 16. Around the age of 17 the final year of schooling provides two routes to the student, either vocational or academic.
- There are 14 universities in Portugal as well as a number of polytechnics.

Spain

Working life: the national provisions

Working week
   Maximum 40 hours a week, nine hours a day. Usual week 40 hours. Shops can set own hours

Public holidays
   13 days

Paid holidays
   30 days minimum. Fifteen days off for marriage; two days off for family death

continued . . .

Minimum wage
> Government sets 'minimum interprofessional salary', reviewed once a year, or after six months if inflation higher than expected

Sick pay
> After first three days, statutory pay is 60% of salary to 20th day, then 75% of salary

Maternity leave
> 16 weeks (18 for twins). Father can take last four weeks as paternity leave. Mothers have one hour off a day to nurse child for first nine months. Parents can work shorter day

Termination
> Notice varies from one to three months. Employees are entitled to 20 days' salary per year worked

Works council
> Every company with 50 or more employees must have a workers' committee, with rights to negotiation, information and consultation

Social protection

- The Spanish scheme is funded partly from employees' and employers' contributions and partly by the state.
- The scheme covers retirement pensions, unemployment benefit, disablement allowances, family benefit, health care and sickness benefit, plus some other areas.
- In 1989 average social protection benefits per head were 1,467 Ecu, one of the lowest figures in the Community.

Health

- The 1978 constitution established the right of every citizen to the protection of health. To this end the health system has developed fairly quickly over the past fifteen years, but not without difficulties.
- Current health care policy aims to reduce social and regional imbalances.
- Private hospitals exist alongside the state system, but represent only a small proportion of health care capacity. In 1987 97.1% of the population was covered by public health care.
- Life expectancy is 78 years for women and 72 for men.
- Spain has one of the highest rates of Aids in the EC at 118.2 cases per million inhabitants. Two-thirds of those cases involve drug addicts.

Education

- Education has undergone a period of rapid change in Spain in recent years. A law passed in 1991 introduced a new system to be gradually implemented during the first half of the 1990s.
- Before 1970 Spanish education was privately based; now there is a system of free and compulsory education from the age of 6 to 16.
- Pre-school education is divided into playschool (age 2–3 years) and kindergarten (age 4–5 years). Both are voluntary and free in public centres. Many playschools are part of day-care centres and belong to businesses, the city councils, private foundations or other private initiatives.
- Enrolment is low at playschool age (10%), but much higher for kindergartens, which are often attached to public or private primary schools.
- Primary schooling is free and compulsory for children aged 6–12.
- Secondary schooling is divided into two phases covering ages 12–15 and 16–17 respectively. At age 15 or 16 the student is then directed towards either intermediate technical training or upper-level secondary schooling.
- The qualifications the students can take at secondary level are the Bachillerato Unificado y Polivalente (BUP) which helps prepare for university studies or the Formación Profesional (technical training).
- To enter university a student must have passed the Curso de Orientación Universitaria (COU), which is an extension of the BUP, and take an entrance exam.
- There are 38 public and four Catholic universities. Half of the universities have been created since 1970.

The United Kingdom

Working life: the national provisions

Working week
> No statutory regulations. In practice factory employees work 37.5–39 hours a week, offices 35–37.5 hours, shops 39 hours

Public holidays
> Eight (10 in Northern Ireland)

Paid holidays
> No statutory requirement to provide holidays. Average 23 days a year. No regulations governing calculation of holiday pay

continued . . .

Minimum wage
> No national minimum. Twenty-six Wages Councils covering 2.5 million workers set minimum hourly and overtime rates for low-paid sectors

Sick pay
> After four days, minimum statutory sick pay is £43.50 ($77), maximum £52.50 ($93)

Maternity leave
> After two years' service, 18 weeks: 90% pay for six weeks, then 12 weeks at £44.50 ($79), plus 22 weeks unpaid, with right to return to work. Less than two years' service, 18 weeks at £44.50 a week, no right to return to work

Termination
> One week's notice for first two years' service; after two years, two weeks, up to maximum of 12 weeks for 12 years' service

Works council
> No workers' councils. No legal requirement to recognize trade unions, for either negotiation or representation

Social protection

- The National Insurance system funded by government and by employees' and employers' contributions, provides a range of benefits including child benefit, retirement pensions, maternity benefit, statutory sick pay, unemployment benefit, widow's and invalidity benefit.
- There is also a form of assistance available for those who have not been able to make adequate contributions.
- In 1988 average social benefits per head were 2,617 Ecu per year.

Health

- All people normally resident in the UK are entitled to use the National Health Service (NHS). No insurance qualification is necessary.
- The NHS is funded by central government and provides hospitals, general practitioners, dentists, and community and school health-care services.
- The 190 district health authorities are responsible for the administration and development of health services within each area.
- Life expectancy is 77.5 years for women and 71.7 years for men.

- The UK has one of the lowest ratios of doctors to inhabitants in the EC at just 1.5 doctors per 1,000 inhabitants. In 1990 there were around 340,000 daily hospital beds available.

Education

- Education is free and compulsory between the ages of 5 and 16.
- There is a large private sector where fees are payable by parents.

Pre-school and primary

- There are both public (free) and private (fee-paying) nurseries for the under–5s.
- Primary schooling covers children aged 5–11.

Middle and secondary

- Some local education authorities operate middle schools which cover the age group of 8–14 years. From middle schools, pupils would go on to senior schools at the age of 12, 13 or 14.
- Some local authorities have retained the grammar-school system with selection by examination at the age of 11; most, however, operate the comprehensive school system with open access to secondary schools for all pupils.
- The age range covered by a secondary school can be either 11–18 or 11–16. If the second route is chosen, pupils can transfer to a sixth-form college at the age of 16.
- At the age of 16 most pupils will take the General Certificate of Secondary Education (GCSE) examination.
- At 16–18 students can choose either to take 'A' levels, which many regard as good preparation for university, or to take vocational courses run by many different organizations such as BTEC, City and Guilds, etc.
- Since 1988 it has been possible for sponsors from business and industry together with the Department for Education to fund the establishment of City Technology Colleges. These are schools for 11–18-year-olds where the curriculum has an emphasis on science and technology.

Tertiary

- The colleges of further education and adult education centres offer a wide variety of both full- and part-time courses.
- There are 43 traditional universities in the UK which have recently been joined by the 29 former polytechnics and 55 colleges of higher education to form the university sector.
- Degree courses last for three or four years. Admission to university will depend upon examination results and probably an interview.

part two

HOW THE EC WORKS

3
The EC treaties

How the EC Developed: A Brief History

The origins of the European Community are to be found in the economic and political history of the period between the First and Second World Wars and in the political and economic structure of Europe after 1945. Between 1918 and 1939 world free trade was increasingly hampered by unilateral actions on the part of countries, the European states in particular, in order to gain temporary economic advantage over their main foreign trade rivals. By taking these actions, which included the imposition of tariffs, quotas and competitive devaluations, they hoped to protect their domestic industries and employment. The inter-war period therefore saw the principle and practice of free trade slowly disappear as a result of these protectionist interventions, all of which progressively weakened the economies of Europe, assisted in the rise of Nazi Germany and contributed in part to the Second World War in 1939–45.

Europe after 1945 was very different from the Europe of the earlier twentieth century. No longer was the world dominated by a few powerful European nation states with overseas colonies; now there were two superpowers, the USSR and the USA. No single European state had either the economic or the military resources to enable it to compete with the USA and USSR on an equal footing.

Drawing on the lessons learnt from the causes of decline of world trade in the inter-war period 1918–39 and the collapse of many European economies as a direct result of the Second World War, attempts were made to foster international cooperation and recovery through a number of newly formed international organizations. The most important of these were:

- The United Nations (UN)
- The International Monetary Fund (IMF)
- The International Bank for Reconstruction and Development (World Bank)
- The General Agreement on Tariffs and Trade (GATT)

All of these, however, were global arrangements with a strong US influence. The nations of Western Europe, none of which retained the economic, political or military status that they had enjoyed prior to 1939,

---

BRUSSELS TREATY ORGANIZATION 1948
The Brussels Treaty was signed in 1948 and related to defence matters. It immediately preceded the North Atlantic Treaty which was signed in 1949. The Brussels Treaty was signed at the beginning of the cold war and at a time when the signatories, Belgium, France, Luxembourg, the Netherlands and the UK, were concerned about a revival of German militarism.

THE COUNCIL OF EUROPE 1949
The Council of Europe (not to be confused with the European Council, part of the organizational structure of the European Community – see chapter 4) was established in 1949 as a means of increasing diplomatic cooperation between its signatories. The competence of the Council was and is very wide but the UK and some other signatories resisted any moves to give the Council supranational rather than intergovernmental powers.

ORGANIZATION FOR EUROPEAN ECONOMIC COOPERATION (OEEC) 1948
The OEEC grew out of the immediate post-war need to distribute aid made available to Europe from the USA as part of the Marshall plan. It was an intergovernmental organization established initially in 1948 and it laid the foundation for the creation of the much wider Organization for Economic Cooperation and Development (OECD), which was set up in 1961.

felt the need for some form of collective arrangement for the mutual protection of their frontiers and for the development of policies to prevent recurrence of the economic rivalries that had existed before 1939. The period up to 1950 consequently saw the establishment of several organizations which, though they had different specific concerns, all shared the aim of encouraging cooperation among West European states.

It was still felt, however, that although the formation of these groupings was a positive step, they could not achieve the objectives of economic growth and the protection of frontiers. It became clear that only by a stronger economic union could real progress be made. Accordingly, during the period 1951–7 negotiations took place which led to the establishment of the European Economic Community, the European Coal and Steel Community and the European Atomic Energy Community.

The decision to proceed in this direction was not, however, a unanimous one; the UK in particular was conspicuous by not being a party to it. British reticence was due in part to the fact that the UK had still a large market for its goods in the remains of its Empire and was not therefore ready to adopt a primarily European perspective on trade. Also, there was a growing belief on mainland Europe that a genuinely workable economic union could not be achieved without a degree of political union and that this would inevitably mean a loss or pooling of sovereignty in certain key areas. Britain was not willing to accept this. The debate concerning federation or a United States of Europe first appeared in a serious form during this period and was to resurface in the 1980s.

The Treaty of Rome (1957)

The original members of the EEC

The Treaty of Rome, which created the European Economic Community and the European Atomic Energy Community, was signed by six countries on 27 March 1957. Membership was not, however, strictly limited to the

---

ORIGINAL SIGNATORIES TO THE TREATY OF ROME
Belgium
France
Italy
Luxembourg
Netherlands
West Germany

Total population: 180 million

founding six member states: 'associate status' membership was created to cater for those countries which had previously enjoyed strong political and economic links with full member states. Countries accorded associate status were able to trade with and obtain aid from the EEC on preferential terms.

Associate members of the EEC

Greece
Israel
Malta
Morocco
Tunisia
Turkey
Spain

Total population: 70 million

The objectives of the Treaty

The Treaty not only set out the policies of the EEC, but also created the institutions which would develop and implement these policies.

Article 2 of the Treaty of Rome states:

The Community shall have as its task by establishing a common market and progressively approximating the economic policies of member states, to promote throughout the Community a harmonious development of economic activities, a continuous and balanced expansion, an increase in stability, an accelerated raising of the standard of living and closer relations between the states belonging to it.

This article clearly reflects the anxieties of the signatories which gave rise to their desire for closer economic and political cooperation.

Article 3 sets out the activities by which the Community would try to achieve the objectives identified in Article 2. The text carefully says that the activities set out shall 'include' the steps mentioned, thus implying that other steps not mentioned in the Treaty may later be taken to promote the development of the Community.

Free trade area or customs union?

The original purpose of the Treaty of Rome was to promote the prosperity and economic expansion of its members by the creation of a customs union.

This meant that all the countries of the Community agreed that in relation to trade with outside countries they would operate a common external tariff.

Once goods enter a country in a customs union from a country outside the union, they move freely within the customs union area without attracting further duty when crossing an internal border. In a free trade area, on the other hand, this concession applies only to goods which are manufactured in that area.

A customs union is therefore surrounded by a 'ring fence' which protects internally produced goods, but ensures that all goods, whether manufactured internally or not, move freely once within the fenced area. Such a policy obviously protects industry and business within the common market it creates.

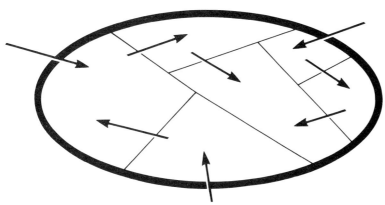

(a) Customs union: once goods enter the union from outside, they are subject to no further duty when crossing national borders within the union

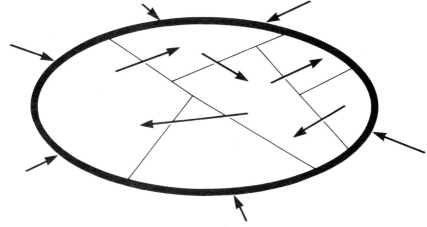

(b) Free trade area: only goods manufactured within the area may cross internal borders without attracting additional duty

Figure 3.1 Customs union or free trade area?

Article 3 of the Treaty of Rome does in fact provide for the elimination of customs duties between member states, but this and several other provisions of the Treaty were not fully adopted or enforced for many years after signature. The impetus for the elimination of customs duties came from the Single European Act and was only finally ensured after 1 January 1993. It is important to understand that the EEC did not originally create a free trade area within its borders.

The new European institutions

The institutions of the Community are examined in detail in chapter 4.

The institutions of the European Economic Community which were created by Article 4 of the Treaty of Rome were a European Parliament, a Council, a Commission and a Court of Justice. The Treaty set out the powers of these institutions and also created an Economic and Social Committee to advise the Council and the Commission and a Court of Auditors to monitor the community's financial affairs.

The Single European Act (1986)

The need for a new Treaty

By the early 1980s the structure of European industry still reflected an uncommon and divided market. For example, different standards applying in different countries forced many countries to manufacture separate products for each national market, thereby preventing them benefiting from economies of scale and so lowering their costs and becoming more profitable. The common market had become, by the early 1980s, the 'uncommon market'. The EC was failing to make effective use of its collective resources and was creating unnecessay costs for buinesses.

THE TREATY OF ROME AS AMENDED BY THE SINGLE EUROPEAN ACT

Part one   Establishes the principles of the European Economic Community

Article 1	Creates the European Economic Community
Article 2	Outlines the task of the Community
Article 3	Sets out a list of activities which the Community shall undertake
Article 4	Creates the institutions

continued . . .

Article 5	Exhorts member states to facilitate and not jeopardize the Treaty objectives
Article 6	States that member states shall coordinate their respective economic policies
Article 7	Enshrines the principle of non-discrimination on the grounds of nationality
Article 8	Gives transitional provisions

Part two Sets out the foundation of the Community

Articles 9–37	Free movement of goods
Articles 38–47	Agriculture
Articles 48–58	Free movement of workers and the right of establishment
Articles 59–66	Freedom to provide services
Articles 67–73	Free movement of capital
Articles 74–84	Transport

Part three Sets out the policies of the Community

Articles 85–90	Competition policy
Article 91	Dumping
Article 92	Aids granted by states
Article 95–99	Tax provisions
Article 99–102	Approximation of Laws
Article 102a–109	Economic policy, conjunctural payments and balance of payments
Articles 110–116	Commercial policy
Articles 117–128	Social policy and the European Social Fund
Articles 129–130	The European Investment Bank
Articles 130a–130e	Economic and social cohesion
Articles 130f–130g	Research and technological development
Articles 130r–130t	Environment

Part four

| Articles 131–136a | Set out the relationship of the Community with associate countries and territories |

Part five   Creates the institutions of the Community

Articles 137–144	The European Parliament
Articles 145–153	The Council
Article 154	is repealed by the SEA
Article 155	The Commission
Articles 156–163	are repealed by the SEA
Articles 164–188	The Court of Justice
Articles 189–192	Common provisions
Articles 193–198	The Economic and Social Committee
Articles 199–209	Financial provisions

Part six

| **Articles 210–247** | General and financial provisions |

The Community realized that without a stronger economic framework, fundamental weaknesses would prevent the EC from achieving the goals of its founders set out in the Treaty of Rome. Moreover, in the increasingly competitive international economic environment, the EC would remain at a disadvantage in relation to its major competitors, Japan and the USA; and as a result of this failure to progress, individual citizens of the member states would be unable to enjoy the economic advantages that should have been theirs.

The development of the SEA

At the beginning of 1985 the newly appointed President of the Commission, Jacques Delors, suggested to the leaders of the member states that steps should be taken to revitalize the Community by removing all non-tariff barriers to trade and attempting to complete the internal market. A summit of EC leaders held in Milan in June 1985 set up an Inter-Governmental Conference to look at the possibility of achieving the single European market by 1992. The basis for discussion was the document published by the Commission in May 1985 entitled *Completing the Internal Market*, which set out a detailed legislative programme and timetable.

The Luxembourg summit in December 1985 resulted in a clear acceptance by all member states that the internal market should be completed by the end of 1992 and that the legal measures necessary should stem from an amendment to the Treaty of Rome which became known as the Single European Act. This Act was ratified by all member states during 1987.

The content of the SEA

THE AIMS OF THE SINGLE EUROPEAN ACT, AS SET OUT IN THE PREAMBLE

1 To continue the work undertaken already and transform relations among member states into a European Union.
2 To implement a common foreign policy.
3 To promote democracy and fundamental rights and freedoms – notably freedom, equality and social justice.
4 To aim at speaking ever increasingly with one voice and to act with consistency and solidarity.
5 To improve the economic and social situation by extending common policies and pursuing new objectives.

The central intention of the Act's architects was that the SEA should provide the necessary political impetus and legal framework to achieve a unified market by 1 January 1993. The Act defined the single market as 'an area without internal frontiers in which the free movement of goods, persons, services and capital is ensured'.

The SEA is a wide-ranging document, covering much more than the single market. It sets out a number of amendments to the original founding treaties and covers subjects such as economic and social cohesion, the environment, cooperation between the various European institutions and greater political cooperation. It also underlines the commitment of the European Community to achieving the aims of the original treaties.

The SEA in action

Since the passing of the Single European Act in 1986 over 80% of more than 300 measures necessary for the creation of the single market have been passed and put into effect. Many steps, however, remain to be taken before the single market is truly complete, even though the arrival of 1 January 1993 marked its official inception. Political problems have lead to deadlock in some key areas, and national administrative systems have not always caught up with policy decisions taken at European level. Some of the issues where difficulties remain are listed in the box on page 100.

THE SINGLE MARKET: PROBLEM AREAS

Customs procedures
Spot checks anywhere within a member state will replace border controls. Restructuring of Customs & Excise departments will be needed before this can be fully implemented.

European company statute
Britain and Germany are both resisting this; Britain objects to the stipulations on worker representation.

European Trademark
The legal mechanisms for this are in place, but the location of the European Trademark office is not yet agreed.

European patent
Has to be agreed by Denmark and Ireland, who need to hold referenda in order to comply with their constitutions.

Takeovers and mergers
Many member states are objecting to proposals made by the Council of Ministers which require the disclosure of company information.

Company taxation
Companies which operate in more than one member state may be taxed twice. Legislation to prevent this still has to be adopted.

The Maastricht Treaty

Background: towards a closer union

The logical extension of many of the principles contained in the Single European Act is an ever closer union, with the influence of the Community reaching more and more deeply into the affairs of the member states. By the late 1980s the pull in this direction had come to be felt particularly strongly on two fronts, towards

- economic and monetary union; and
- political union, including a common foreign and security policy.

Not all the member states were equally enthusiastic about this trend. Britain, under the premiership of Mrs Thatcher, was notable for its reservations, favouring a looser, wider, grouping incorporating a larger number of member states. Others, however – the so-called 'federalists', who included the President of the Commission, Jacques Delors – believed that the time had come to consolidate and deepen the ties among the existing members, to develop more common policies and more powerful Community institutions to promote and enforce them.

THE MAASTRICHT TREATY, 1: OBJECTIVES

Article A
The creation of a European union of states founded on the European communities and added to by the provisions of this treaty

Article B
- The creation of an area without internal frontiers
- The strengthening of economic and social cohesion
- The establishment of economic and monetary union
- Ultimately the creation of a single currency
- The implementation of a common foreign and security policy
- The introduction of citizenship of the European union
- The development of close cooperation in justice and home affairs

Article C
The institutions of the European Community shall continue to serve the European union and ensure the consistency of its policies

Article D
The European Council which comprises the heads of government shall instigate measures to promote the European union and define its political direction

Article E
Confirms that the institutions of the European Community shall continue to exercise their responsibilities as before and shall receive additional and modified responsibilities under this treaty

Article F
Confirms the respect the signatories have for the national identity of member states and human rights within them as agreed by the European Convention on Human Rights

---

At summit meetings of the Community members' heads of government in Strasbourg (December 1989) and Dublin (June 1990) it was decided that two intergovernmental conferences should be convened: one on

economic and monetary union and one on political union, to consider a
new Community Treaty. The ensuing debate began in Rome in December
1990 and concluded in Maastricht in December 1991.

The problem of ratification

On 11 December 1991 the European Community leaders agreed the text of
a Treaty on European Union and Economic and Monetary Union – known
as the Maastricht Treaty from the place where agreement was reached. The
member states agreed that in order to take effect, the Treaty would have to
be ratified by each individual country according to its own constitutional
procedures.

The constitutions of Denmark, France and Ireland require that a
referendum is held to confirm or reject the government's decision to adopt
any measure with constitutional significance for the country. The
Maastricht Treaty, with far-reaching implications for the national
independence of the EC member states (see below) was therefore subject to
a referendum in each of these three countries.

While the voters in France and Ireland approved the Treaty, albeit by
fairly narrow majorities, those of Denmark rejected it in the referendum
held on 2 June 1992. The Danish government conducted a campaign
designed to change the voters' minds, and a second referendum on 18 May
1993 resulted in a 'yes' vote.

In Britain, where opinion on the future of the Community was sharply
divided, calls for a referendum on ratification of the Treaty were firmly
rejected by the government of John Major, which maintained that under
the British constitution it was for the government to take responsibility for
its treaty contracts.

The Treaty will come into force throughout all member states on the first
day of the month after the last signatory state has ratified it.

Maastricht: its scope and importance

Asked why the Maastricht Treaty was so important, the Commission
President Jacques Delors identified five main reasons (see *The European*, 17
September 1992):

- That it would give Europe the strength essential for success in world
  markets
- That it would foster peacable relations in a working society that was
  increasingly fragmented
- That the Community must move forward, escaping the stagnation
  that has beset it in the past
- That through this Treaty member states will be more closely involved
  in Community affairs
- That without the Maastricht Treaty the future of the Community
  and of Europe as a whole is uncertain and dangerous

The crucial point about the Maastricht Treaty is that it extends the scope of the Community into areas that have hitherto been exclusively the province of national governments. Some of these areas are incorporated into the institutional framework established by the Treaty of Rome; some, such as the common foreign and security policy, remain outside the formal institutional base of the EC.

Other important general points about the Treaty are:

- It creates a common policy on judicial affairs
- It gives added emphasis to the European Council of Heads of Government as the major force for future policy-making
- It gives the European Parliament increased powers of decision-making and inquiry and increased rights to be consulted

---

THE MAASTRICHT TREATY, 2: AMENDMENTS TO THE TREATY OF ROME

The term 'European Economic Community' shall be replaced by 'European Community'

Article 2 of the Treaty of Rome shall be replaced by a new wider Article 2 which encompasses the promotion of a harmonious and balanced development of economic activities, sustainable and non-inflationary growth, respecting the environment, a high degree of convergence of economic performance, a high level of employment and social protection, the raising of the standard of living and quality of life, and economic and social cohesion and solidarity among member states

Article 3
A new Article 3, replacing the previous Article 3 of the Treaty of Rome, provides that the activities of the Community shall include the provisions set out below, which shall be implemented within the agreed timetable

Article 3A
This is an addition to the Treaty of Rome and provides:
1   For the adoption by the Community of an economic policy based on the close coordination of member states' economic policies on the internal market and the definition of common objectives
2   This shall include the irrevocable fixing of exchange rates, the introduction of a single currency – the Ecu – and a single monetary and exchange rate policy

continued . . .

3 Member states shall comply with certain guiding principles as to stable prices, sound public finances and monetary conditions, and a sustainable balance of payments:

(a) The elimination as between member states of customs duties and quantitative restrictions on the import and export of goods and of all other measures having equivalent effect

(b) A common commercial policy

(c) An internal market characterized by the abolition, as between member states, of obstacles to the free movements of goods, persons, services and capital

(d) Measures concerning the entry and movement of persons in the internal market as provided for in Article 100C

(e) A common policy in the sphere of agriculture and fisheries

(f) A common policy in the sphere of transport

(g) A system ensuring that competition in the internal market is not distorted

(h) The approximation of the laws of member states to the extent required for the functioning of the common market

(i) A policy in the social sphere comprising a European Social Fund

(j) The strengthening of economic and social cohesion

(k) A policy in the sphere of the environment

(l) The strengthening of the competitiveness of Community industry

(m) The promotion of research and technological development

(n) Encouragement for the establishment and development of trans-European networks

(o) A contribution to the attainment of a high level of health protection

(p) A contribution to education and training of quality and to the flowering of the cultures of the member states

(q) A policy in the sphere of development cooperation

(r) The association of the overseas countries and territories in order to increase trade and promote jointly economic and social development

(s) A contribution to the strengthening of consumer protection

(t) Measures in the spheres of energy, civil protection and tourism

continued . . .

Article 3B (Subsidiarity)

A new Article which seeks to establish that the European Community should not pass legal rules where the same result can be achieved by member states themselves passing legislation. In other words, the principle of subsidiarity is now part of the constitution of the Community and the Community shall not pass any rules which go beyond what is necessary to achieve the objectives of the Treaty

Article 4

Confirms the institution of the European Community and creates, as well as the Economic and Social Committee, a committee of the regions to act in an advisory capacity

Article 4A

Provides for the establishment of the European system of central banks and the European Central Bank

Subsidiarity

The text of the Treaty reflects the compromise reached after lengthy and difficult debate between the 'federalists' and those who resisted any further encroachment of European powers on national affairs – whom one might call the 'nationalists'. A key concept in reaching this compromise was that of 'subsidiarity', by which is meant that decisions should be taken as close to the point of impact as possible, and that any action by the Community shall not go beyond what is necessary to achieve the objectives of the Treaty (see box, Article 3B).

The compromise between 'federalists' and 'nationalists' is encapsulated in a phrase from Article of the Treaty itself:

This Treaty marks a new stage in the process of creating an ever closer union among the peoples of Europe, where decisions are taken as closely as possible to the citizens.

4

The institutions of the Community

The European Commission

Composition

The seventeen Commissioners are nominated by the governments of the member states. The larger states nominate two commissioners each, others one each, as follows:

- France, Germany, Italy, Spain and the UK: two commissioners each
- Belgium, Denmark, Greece, Ireland, Luxembourg, the Netherlands, Portugal: one commissioner each

The members of the Commission are technically appointed by the European Council. Attempts in the past by the President of the Commission to influence the nominations have been strongly resisted. Any alteration in the total number of Commissioners can be decided only by unanimous decision of the European Council.

Each commissioner holds office for four years, after which he or she may be replaced by another appointee or reappointed for a further four years.

The President and six Vice Presidents of the Commission are elected by the European Council from the body of the Commission. They hold office for two years, which may be renewed.

THE COMMISSION (1992)

Jacques Delors	France	President
René Steichen	Luxembourg	Agriculture
Kavel Van Miert	Belgium	Competition policy
Raniero Vanni D'Archirafi	Italy	Internal market financial services, small firms
Padraig Flynn	Ireland	Social affairs, employment, immigration
Ioannis Paleokrasses	Greece	Environmental policy, nuclear safety, fisheries
Antonio Roberti	Italy	Research and development
Hans van den Broek	Netherlands	Foreign and security policy, enlargement
Bruce Millan	UK	Regional policy
Sir Leon Brittan	UK	Trade policy
Peter Schmidhuber	Germany	Budget
Henning Christophersen	Denmark	Economic affairs
Manuel Marin	Spain	Development policy
Christianne Scrivener	France	Consumer affairs and taxation
Abel Matutes	Spain	Energy and transport
Joao Deus Pinteiro	Portugal	Relations with the European Parliament and external relations
Martin Bangemann	Germany	Industrial policy

Functions

The functions and powers of the Commission, as set out in Article 155 of the Treaty of Rome, are:

- to ensure that the provisions of the Treaty are applied
- to formulate recommendations or deliver opinions
- to decide and participate in the shaping of measures taken by the Council and the European Parliament
- to exercise the powers conferred on it by the Council.

The Commission is responsible for the implementation of Community policy. It may also initiate Community policy by putting items on the agenda for discussion by the Council of Ministers.

Each Commissioner is responsible for a particular area of Community policy. Each policy area has a Director-General and staff to carry out and oversee the implementation of policy (see box).

In essence the Commission is there to protect the interests of the Community, and accordingly Commissioners are required to act in the interests of the Commission and not in the interests of individual countries or the governments which appoint them. In the course of promoting and protecting Community interests, the Commission may bring an action against a member state if it considers there has been a breach of an obligation of the Treaty. Article 169 of the Treaty of Rome states:

If the Commission considers that a member state has failed to fulfil an obligation under this Treaty, it shall deliver a reasoned opinion on the matter after giving the state concerned the opportunity to submit its observations. If the state concerned does not comply with the opinion within the period laid down by the Commission the latter may bring the matter before the Court of Justice.

Figure 4.1 The European Commission
Source: *European Commission*

DIRECTORATES-GENERAL OF EUROPEAN COMMUNITY

1 External relations
2 Economic and financial affairs
3 Internal market and industrial affairs
4 Competition
5 Employment, social affairs and education
6 Agriculture
7 Transport
8 Development
9 Personnel and administration
10 Information, communication and culture
11 Environment, consumer protection and nuclear safety
12 Science, research and development
13 Telecommunications, information industry and innovation
14 Fisheries
15 Financial institutions and company law
16 Regional policy
17 Energy
18 Credit and investments
19 Budget
20 Financial control
21 Customs union and indirect taxation
22 Coordination of structural instruments
23 Small and medium-sized enterprises

Part of the reason for the provision of this power is to ensure that the custody of the policies and practices of the Community is in the hands of a neutral body, and that the guardianship of the Treaties is not left to individual member states.

In practice some 75% of cases brought under Article 169 are settled by agreement between member states and the Commission and no hearing before the European Court of Justice is necessary.

Following the ratification of the Maastricht Treaty, increased powers to be given to the Court of Justice will permit it to fine member states for non-compliance with its rulings.

The UK has been the subject of many complaints to the Commission, some of which have resulted in actions under Article 169. The most common areas of complaint are

- equal opportunities for men and women
- environmental matters and
- fisheries matters.

THE COMMISSIONER'S OATH

I solemnly undertake:

- To perform my duties in complete independence, in the general interests of the Communities
- In carrying out my duties, neither to seek nor to take instructions from any government or body
- To refrain from any action incompatible with my duties
- I formally note the undertaking of each member state to respect this principle and not to seek to influence members of the Commission in the performance of their task
- I further undertake to respect, both during and after my term of office, the obligations arising therefrom, and in particular the duty to behave with integrity and discretion as regards the acceptance, after I have ceased to hold office, of certain appointments or benefits

The most famous recent case involving the UK under Article 169 was *Commission* v. *UK re Merchant Shipping Rules* (Case 246/89R). This case was part of the group of cases which arose out of the British government's introduction of rules which prohibited non-UK registered vessels from fishing in British waters. The new rules prohibited foreign owners to register their boats as British and thereby bypass the prohibition (see chapter 5). The European Court of Justice ordered the suspension of the Merchant Shipping Act pending the full hearing, thus confirming the supremacy of Community over domestic law and leading to the headline in *The European* on 26 July 1991: 'Spanish Fishermen 1; British Sovereignty 0'.

The European Council

Composition

The European Council consists of the heads of government of the Community member states. This group meets usually twice a year; these meetings are often called the 'European summits'.

Functions

The European Council deliberates on matters of high strategy with respect to the development of the Community, particularly steps towards closer integration. Issues for discussion may be put on the Council's agenda by members of the European Council itself or by the Commission.

The Council's decisions or recommendations may be either sent on to the Commission for implementation, or referred to the Parliament (see below) for an opinion; in the latter case, the European Council is not bound to act in accordance with the Parliament's opinion.

The Commission

Makes proposals

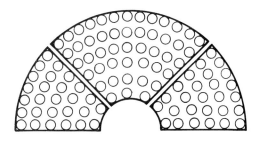

The European Parliament

Gives opinions and proposes amendments

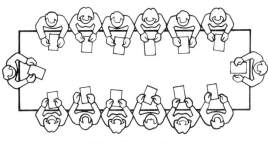

The Council

Makes decisions

Figure 4.2 The three central institutions of the Community

The Council of Ministers

The Council of Ministers is an entirely separate body from the European Council. Its membership varies, as it consists of the minister from each member state with national responsibility for whatever area of activity is under discussion. Thus, for example, the Council of Ministers may consist at one time of the Agriculture Ministers of all the member states, and at another of all the Ministers for Home Affairs, Ministers of the Interior, the British Home Secretary, etc.

   The Council of Ministers is envisaged by the Community Treaties as the body responsible for the formulation of Community policy. Using the same example, the Council of Agriculture Ministers would deliberate on and draw up agricultural policy, and the Council of Home Affairs Ministers would address questions of immigration or crime policy.

The Committee of Permanent Representatives (COREPER)

The Maastricht Treaty created a new Article 151 in the Treaty of Rome by which the Committee of Permanent Representatives was brought into being. This body is responsible for preparing the work of the Council of Ministers and carrying out tasks assigned to it by the Council of Ministers.

Qualified majority voting

The Single European Act of 1986 introduced the principle of qualified majority voting or QMV (see box) for use in circumstances where the Council of Ministers found itself unable to reach unanimous agreement on a policy measure. The introduction of this system has enabled the Community to make progress on issues which before 1986 would have been totally blocked by the dissension of one or two member states.

   Many articles of the Treaty of Rome originally required decisions of the Council of Ministers to be unanimous and some still do. Such articles include

- the admission of a new member
- the location of the institutions of the Community and
- fiscal measures.

The Single European Act extended the provision of QMV to cover matters necessary for the completion of the single market. Other non-single-market issues remained subject to the right of veto which was established by virtue of the 'Luxembourg compromise' in 1966. This informal agreement between member states gives an individual right of veto to a member state where 'very important interests' of that member state were at stake.

QUALIFIED MAJORITY VOTING

This is a system of weighted voting whereby the Council of
Ministers can in certain circumstances make decisions even if not
all states are in agreement. Each state is allocated a number of
votes as follows:

Belgium	5
Denmark	3
France	10
Germany	10
Greece	5
Ireland	3
Italy	10
Luxembourg	3
Netherlands	5
Portugal	5
Spain	8
UK	10
Total	77 votes

The weightings were drawn up to reflect the relative populations
of member states. A majority is at least 54 votes cast by at least
eight members.

The Commission was criticized in the run-up to 1992 for including in
the single market programme measures which might not naturally have
found themselves there in order to take advantage of the QMV provision.

The European Parliament

Composition

The Parliament, which is based in Strasbourg, consists of 518 members
directly elected by the voters of each member state. The number of seats
allocated to each country is shown in the box.

Elections have taken place every five years since 1979; the last elections
were held in 1989 and the next are due to be held in 1994. The first direct
elections to the Parliament took place in 1979; before this date the
Assembly (as it was known before the Single European Act) consisted of
142 delegates *chosen* from the national parliaments of member states.

Once elected to the Parliament, members (MEPs) align themselves with their party groupings, not according to the countries they represent. Thus, for example, British Labour MEPs, French Socialist members and German Social Democrats would all consider themselves part of the Socialist grouping. Obviously, because the precise orientations of analogous parties differ from country to country, these groupings are less homogeneous than any national political party.

A President and 12 Vice-Presidents are elected by the members for a two-year term. The President takes the chair at the plenary sessions of the Parliament and, together with the Vice-Presidents (who are generally referred to as The Bureau), he is responsible for the organization of the work of the Parliament. The Bureau determines how work is to be conducted and decides on the membership and organization of the 18 standing committees of the Parliament where much of the detailed work is carried out. Broadly these committees correspond to the Directorates-General of the Commission.

THE EUROPEAN PARLIAMENT, 1: COMPOSITION

Country	No. of seats
Belgium	24
Denmark	16
France	81
Germany	81
Greece	24
Ireland	15
Italy	81
Luxembourg	6
Netherlands	25
Portugal	24
Spain	60
UK	81
Total seats	518

The Parliament is supported by a secretariat, which was originally based in Luxembourg. The plenary sessions of Parliament are however held in Strasbourg, except in April, June and October, when they are held in Luxembourg. Not surprisingly the Parliament feels the need for some permanent staff to be located in Brussels. Most MEPs regard the present arrangement as highly unsatisfactory, and it has been estimated that it takes up some 244,700 hours of staff time every year merely to travel, pack, unpack and organize the business of the Parliament in this way. This costs the European taxpayer an estimated £100 million every year.

Figure 4.3 The European Parliament
Source: *European Parliament Photo Library*

THE EUROPEAN PARLIAMENT, 2: RESULTS OF LAST ELECTION (1989)	
Party grouping	*No. of seats gained*
Socialist	180 (including 46 British Labour MEPs)
Christian Democrats	121
Liberals, Democrats and Reformists	49
Communists and Allies	42
European Democratic Group	34 (includes 32 British Conservative MEPs)
Greens	30
European Democratic Alliance	20
European Right	17
Rainbow Group	13
Independents	12

Functions and Powers

It is important to understand that the European Parliament does not have the law-making function of a national parliament. The Treaty of Rome speaks in terms of 'advisory and supervisory powers'. However, over the years the Parliament has gained additional power by virtue of decisions of the European Court of Justice and amendments to the original Treaty provisions.

The Single European Act enhanced the consultative role of the Parliament; also, Article 6 provides that the Council of Ministers and the Parliament shall cooperate on the introduction of measures to implement the single market.

The Maastricht Treaty gives significant additional power to the Parliament under Article 138:

- it gives the Parliament, for the first time, the power of veto over proposals for legislation in some areas;
- it creates an arbitration procedure for occasions when the Council of Ministers and the Parliament cannot agree on legislative proposals.

The European Court of Justice

Figure 4.4 The European Court of Justice
Source: *Court of Justice of the European Communities*

Composition

The Court consists of 13 judges appointed by the governments of the member states. The Treaty of Rome does not provide that each member state shall have a judge in the Court, but this has become customary. The thirteenth judge (who exists to ensure that the court cannot divide equally) is traditionally appointed in rotation from the UK, Germany, France and Italy.

In practice, only on the most important cases will all judges sit on a case. For routine cases and for the purpose of making preliminary recommendations the judges divide into groups of three or six known as 'chambers'.

The Advocates General, of whom there are six, four chosen from the larger member states and two representing the smaller states, are equal in status to the judges. Their main function is to assist the judges by giving an opinion prior to that of the court itself. Advocates General give opinions individually and in general, the court will not always follow their recommendations.

Functions

The function and powers of the European Court of Justice are set out in Articles 169–81 of the Treaty of Rome. The Court has jurisdiction (*inter alia*)

For more on the operation of the European Court of Justice, see chapter 5

- to hear cases between member states where there has been a failure to fulfil the requirements of the Treaty
- to hear action brought by the Commission against member states for breaches of the Treaty
- to hear action brought by member states against the institutions of the Community for infringement or misuse of their powers
- under Article 177, to give preliminary rulings on the interpretation of the Treaty.

In addition, the Maastricht Treaty gives the Court the power to fine member states who do not implement legislation within designated time scales.

The European Court of First Instance

Composition

The Court consists of 12 members, one from each member state, who elect from among their number a President who serves for a renewable term of three years.

Functions

The purpose of the Court of First Instance, which was established by the Single European Act, is primarily to reduce the workload of the European Court of Justice.

The Court has jurisdiction (*inter alia*)

- to hear disputes between the Community and its employees;
- to hear action against the institutions of the Community brought by member states or other persons or institutions on the grounds of misuse of power, lack of competence or breach of procedure.

The Court of Auditors

The Court of Auditors was instituted in 1975 by the Budgetary Powers Treaty. Twelve members are nominated, one by each member state, for a six-year term which may be renewed.

The Court of Auditors, as its name implies, has the task of auditing the accounts of the various institutions and bodies of the Community. Unlike business auditors, its remit is not simply to check that expenditure has been properly incurred and can be accounted for, but, like the UK Audit Commission, that unnecessary waste has not occurred.

It was this latter point that led the Court to criticize the other institutions of the Community for the huge costs of maintaining diverse locations for Community institutions.

The Economic and Social Committee

There are 188 members of the Economic and Social Committee allocated as set out in the box below.

Belgium	12	Italy	24
Denmark	9	Luxembourg	6
France	24	Netherlands	12
Germany	24	Portugal	12
Greece	24	Spain	12
Ireland	9	UK	24

The function of the Committee is to advise the Council and the Commission and to prepare opinions on matters that it thinks are important in the economic and social fields.

Members of the Committee are appointed for four years by the Council of Ministers from a cross-section of the general public nominated by member states. The Committee elects its own Chair who holds office for two years.

The Maastricht Treaty, without giving explicit additional powers to the Committee, does provide that it shall be consulted by the Council and Commission on those matters where the scope of the Community is extended, such as Trans-European Networks, consumer protection etc.

For details of these policies, see chapter 8

The Regional Committee

The Regional Committee was established in 1975 as a means of promoting the development of the poorer and usually less geographically accessible regions of the community. The Committee comprises senior civil servants from member states with administraive support from the Commission. The Committee operates the Regional Development Fund and, under the provision of the Maastricht Treaty, is entitled to be consulted on such matters as Trans-European Networks.

The European Investment Bank

The European Investment Bank (EIB) was created by Articles 129 and 130 of the Treaty of Rome. Its headquarters are in Luxembourg.

Composition

- The Board of Governors consists of one minister from each member state. It meets once a year.
- The Board of Directors consists of members nominated by individual states and meets at least 12 times a year. It has responsibility for approving loans and the terms of those loans.
- The Management Committee makes recommendations to the Board of Directors as to whether loans should be made and implements the Directors' decisions. It is responsible for the day-to-day running of the EIB.

Functions

Under Article 130 of the Treaty the EIB is empowered to ensure 'the balanced and steady development of the Community' by means of providing loans or loan guarantees to member states for projects which will enable individual member states to work towards EC goals.

Certain conditions have to be met before the EIB will grant loan finance:

- The loan must in some way contribute to economic growth in one or more of the poorer members of the EC.
- whilst contributing to economic growth it must also assist in enabling the Community as a whole to work towards the accomplishment of a common policy, e.g. transport/energy objectives.
- It must also contribute towards enhancing the competitiveness of EC industry.
- In financial terms the project must not be expected to make a loss. There must be provision of adequate security so that in the event of the project not being successful, the EIB does not incur losses. Interest rates are lower than ruling market rates, thereby encouraging investment in projects with relatively low rates of return.

The EIB obtains its loan capital from two sources: contributions from EC members and the financial markets.

5

Community law

This chapter covers:
- The distinction between procedural law and substantive law
- The distinction between Community law and domestic (or national) law
- The relationship between Community law and British domestic law
- The nature of sovereignty
- When individuals may have recourse to Community law in a national court: 'direct effect'
- 'Secondary' legislation: regulations, directives and decisions
- The operation of the European Court of Justice

Introduction: Some Distinctions

European Community law is a complicated area and it can seem difficult to explain any one of the fundamental concepts without referring to others equally in need of explanation. However, before any understanding of EC law can be reached it is essential to grasp some basic distinctions, namely between:

- procedural and substantive law
- Community and domestic (or national) law
- primary and secondary law

Procedural law and substantive law

- Procedural laws are those which relate to how law is made, how legal rules relate to each other, how they work and how they are applied.

- Substantive laws are those which give effect to the policy decisions of the legislators.

The law of the European Community contains both procedural and substantive elements. The Treaties that establish what the Community is and how it works, that set up the constitition of the Community and define the relationships between the Community as an instition and the member states, constitute procedural law. The rules that set out in detail what Community policies are in various areas and how they are to be implemented in the member states constitute substantive law.

Community law and national law

The laws of the European Community, as created by the Treaties and related Community legislation, are distinct from the body of law enacted by the legislature of each individual member state. This latter is called either 'national law' or 'domestic law'.

We shall see below that there are areas in which the relative priority of Community and national law becomes a matter for dispute. None the less, the possibility of such conflict does not arise in all areas of public and private life: while national law may from time to time have to be changed by the governments of the member states to bring it into line with Community law, there are many areas of national law that remain relatively untouched by a country's membership of the EC. Criminal law and matrimonial law are two examples of this.

Primary and secondary legislation

Many textbooks divide Community laws into primary and secondary legislation: the Treaty provisions that establish the legal framework of the Community and set out its basic policies and principles of operation are primary legislation, whereas the rules of various kinds by which those policies are implemented are secondary legislation.

This is a useful way of classifying Community law, and one that is used in this chapter. However, it is essential to grasp that no hierarchical distinction is involved; that is, secondary legislation is in no way inferior to or less powerful than primary legislation.

A Cautionary Note!

It is important not to confuse primary and secondary sources of European Community law with procedural and substantive law. The primary sources of law are, as we have said, contained in the Treaties, mainly the Treaty of Rome and its subsequent amendments. But the rules contained here are not all procedural. Article 119, for example, provides that men and women shall receive equal pay for equal work. This is a substantive legal rule.

Similarly, Directives and Regulations, secondary sources of law, may lay down procedural rules; for example, Directive 76/207, which guarantees equal treatment, requires member states to exercise their rights via due process of law, in other words to give individuals rights of access to the courts, if necessary, to challenge any failure to implement the legal rule concerned.

Primary Legislation: The Treaties

The Treaties are usually referred to as primary sources of law, in the sense that although they do not for the most part contain detailed legal rules they are where we find the basic legal principles of the Community. The Treaties which make up the Community (see box) can be thought of as the Community's constitution: they state what the major policies of the community are and they establish in broad terms by what means those policies can be put into practice.

For more detail on the Treaty of Rome, the Single European Act and the Maastricht Treaty, see chapter 3.

THE COMMUNITY TREATIES

The Treaty of Rome (1957)
The Merger Treaty (1965)
The Acts of Accession of the various member states (UK 1972)
Budgetary Treaties (1970 and 1975)
The Single European Act (1986)
The Treaty on European Union (The Maastricht Treaty) 1992

Community Law and Domestic Law

In order for a country to join the European Community its head of state must sign the Treaty of Rome. However, when a sovereign state signs an international treaty it does not necessarily follow that the provisions of that treaty automatically become part of the domestic law of that state; that is, they cannot necessarily be enforced in the national courts of that state.

Dualism

The UK constitution regards international law and domestic law as two entirely separate legal systems. The subjects of international law are sovereign states; the subjects of domestic law are individuals. According to this theory, individuals cannot be the subject of international law. This approach is called 'dualism', and is adhered to by the UK.

For example, the European Convention on Human Rights (an international treaty) was signed by the UK in 1950. It has never been enacted by the British parliament as a national law. It is therefore not possible for an individual to stand up in a domestic court in the UK and claim his or her rights under the Convention directly. If there is no remedy under any domestic legal rule to help, the only redress is to the European Court of Human Rights (not to be confused with the European Court of Justice), the authority set up by the Convention with jurisidiction in the area of human rights.

SOVEREIGNTY: WHAT IS IT?

What is a sovereign state?
A sovereign state is one which has the power to make its own legal rules and political decisions without reference to any other controlling state. Like individuals sovereign states may voluntarily enter agreements which may limit their powers to act as they wish.

What is parliamentary sovereignty?
Parliamentary sovereignty is the right of the legislature (parliament) to make and repeal whatever legal rules it wishes. The UK constitution does not allow for any parliament to pass a legal rule which cannot in theory by replaced by any subsequent parliament.

When a national legislature passes a law that cannot be repealed in the normal way it is said to have 'entrenched' that piece of legislation. This is a procedure often used by those countries with written constitutions in order to ensure that to change a constitutional rule is a more serious and more difficult step than to change an 'ordinary' piece of legislation.

The European Communities Act 1972: 'hooking in' the Treaty of Rome

Because of Britain's adherence to dualism, in order for the Treaty of Rome to be made part of domestic law in the UK it was necessary for the UK to pass a domestic Act of Parliament. This was the European Communities Act of 1972. This piece of legislation can be regarded as a 'hook' which brings the Treaty of Rome into national law.

Section 2(1) of the European Communities Act 1972, which gives effect to the Treaty of Rome in UK law, reads as follows:

A ll such rights, powers, liabilities, obligations and restrictions from time to time created or arising by or under the Treaties, or in accordance with the Treaties, are without further enactment to be given legal effect or used in the UK and shall be recognised and available in law and shall be enforced, allowed and followed accordingly; and the expression 'enforceable Community right' and similar expressions shall be read as referring to one to which this subsection applies.

It is important to understand, however, that the European Communities Act is only an ordinary Act of Parliament, just like any other. It has not been 'entrenched' (see box) – indeed, there is no means of doing this in the UK constitution. From a strictly legal point of view, therefore, the Act can be repealed with as much ease as, say, the Road Traffic Act. That doesn't mean, of course, that there wouldn't be enormous political and economic obstacles to repealing the Act; but in theory it could be done.

To recap . . .

So, if we sum up at this point, we find:

- That according to UK law only states (and some international organizations) – not individuals – are the subjects of international law.

- That in order to become a member of the European Community, a member state must sign the Treaty of Rome and go through any procedures required by its own constitution to bring the provisions of the Treaty into domestic law.

- That even after the Treaty of Rome was implemented in UK law by the passing of the European Communities Act, it is not the case that all the provisions of the Treaty can be claimed by individuals in domestic courts; they cannot. However, some provisions of the Treaty of Rome do give rights to individuals which can be claimed in national courts; this point is discussed in more detail below.

- That in effect, therefore, the European Community has created a set of legal rules which are both (a) international and bind member states on the one hand, and (b) domestic and bind and give rights to individuals on the other.

In an early case (*Costa* v. *ENEL* – Case 6/64 1964 (ECR) 585) the European Court of Justice had this to say about Community law and its relationship with domestic law:

By contrast with ordinary international Treaties the EEC Treaty has created its own legal system, which on the entry into force of the Treaty, becomes an integral part of the legal systems of the member states and which their courts are bound to apply. By creating a community of unlimited duration having . . . powers stemming from a limitation of sovereignty, or a transfer of powers from the states to the community, the member states have limited their sovereign rights, albeit with limited fields, and have thus created a body of law which binds both their nationals and themselves.

Two further questions immediately arise:

- What is the relationship between European Community laws on the one hand and domestic laws on the other, and what happens in the event of a conflict between the two?
- Can individuals claim rights given by the Treaties in national courts and how do we know which these rights are?

Community law and domestic law: which takes priority?

Article 5 of the Treaty of Rome states:

Member states shall take all appropriate measures, whether general or particular, to ensure fulfilment of the obligations arising out of this Treaty or resulting from action taken by the institutions of the community. They shall facilitate the achievement of the community's tasks.

They shall abstain from any measure which would jeopardise the attainment of the objectives of this Treaty.

In addition, S.2(4) of the European Communities Act 1972 speaks of giving effect to any enactment (of the Community) passed *or to be passed*.

All of this would seem to indicate that in effect the law-making power of future UK parliaments was limited in 1972 by the then parliament and that law-making from that date must be construed in the light of Community law. We can see how this takes place in practice by studying the example of the Spanish Fisheries cases (see box). This episode demonstrated not only that the UK courts have the power to interpret UK law so that it does not conflict with Community law, but that they can actually suspend Acts of Parliament which do so conflict. It is therefore apparent that parliament's law-making capacity has indeed been limited by membership of the Community.

On the other hand, should parliament wish to withdraw from the Community then the European Communities Act 1972 could be repealed. It might help to imagine the situation as similar to that when a person joins a club, agreeing as a condition of admittance not to do anything now or in the future which conflicts with membership, but not thereby giving away the right to leave the club if so desired. Preliminary sovereignty is suspended but not given away.

The Spanish Fisheries cases

In 1988 the UK parliament passed the Merchant Shipping Act. The aim of this Act was to safeguard the British inshore fishing fleet. The Community common fisheries policy sets strict catch quotas for each national fishing fleet and Spanish owners were registering their vessels as British in order to gain a share in the British quota. The Act attempted to prevent registration as British any fishing vessel owned by a foreign national. Some 95 Spanish trawlers were affected.

One of the cornerstones of Community policy is the freedom of establishment, which gives every Community national the right to establish him- or herself as a self-employed person in another member state. The Act effectively prevented non-UK nationals from setting up in business as trawler operators in the UK.

Owners of the Spanish vessels unable to register under the new legislation challenged its validity. Using the Article 177 procedure (see below), the matter was referred to the European Court of Justice.

Pending the result of their hearing, however, a dispute arose as to whether in the meantime the Spanish vessels could continue to fish. The House of Lords (the UK's highest court) had to decide whether or not it could temporarily suspend the operation of the Merchant Shipping Act, pending the European Court of Justice's judgment. This in turn became a matter for the European Court of Justice, which held that the House of Lords could suspend the law.

The Merchant Shipping Act was repealed, in part as a result of an action by the Commission against the UK government.

Individuals and Community law: 'direct effect'

The second question we identified is whether, as the Treaty of Rome has been 'hooked' into national law, an individual citizen can go to a national court and claim his rights under the Treaty.

Not all provisions of the Treaty give such individual rights; those which can be used in this way are said to have 'direct effect.'

The European Court of Justice decided in 1962 that some provisions of the Treaty of Rome do have direct effect, and in the case of *Van Gend en Loos* (Case 26/62) it set out the test which determines whether an individual treaty provision is directly effective. In order to have direct effect, a Treaty provision must be:

- clear and unambiguous;
- unconditional; and
- capable of taking effect without further action by either the Community or a member state.

This rule has proved valuable in many situations where individuals have felt that their rights, e.g. as to free movement or equal treatment, have been infringed, and it has given them a way of claiming their rights in their own domestic courts (see box for an example).

Treaty provisions are sometimes stated to have *horizontal or vertical direct effect*. This is less confusing than it sounds.

Treaty provisions may impose obligations on member states which can be enforced against that member state by an individual; these provisions are said to have *vertical* direct effect. Some Treaty provisions may create rights which an individual can claim against another individual; these provisions are said to have *horizontal* direct effect.

DEFRENNE V. SABENA (NO.2) (CASE 43/75)

Article 119 of the Treaty of Rome is the equal treatment provision. It provides that men and women should receive equal pay for equal work.

The reasoning behind this is not only that of social equality, but also that member states and companies that implement equal pay should not be at a competitive disadvantage compared to those member states and organizations where it is implemented.

Miss Defrenne sued her former employers, the Belgian airline Sabena, for compensation for their failure to pay air hostesses and male cabin stewards equally.

The provisions of Article 119 comply with the test in *Van Gend en Loos* and have direct effect. Miss Defrenne's claim in her own national court was therefore successful.

The two European cases which establish the existence of vertical and horizontal direct effect are the two already mentioned in this section.

- In *Van Gend en Loos* (Case 26/62), the Court established that the actions of the Dutch public authorities could be challenged by an individual company in respect of customs duty placed on glue. This is vertical direct effect.
- *Defrenne v Sabena* (No.2) (Case 43/75), set out in the box, shows an individual claiming rights under the Treaty against another individual. This is horizontal direct effect.

Secondary Legislation: Regulations, Directives, Decisions

It is through so-called 'secondary' legislation that the European Community puts into place the thousands of detailed rules which are necessary for the operation of the Community and the single market. It is also through the secondary legislation that the domestic laws of member states are harmonized where this is deemed to be important or necessary for the operation of the Community.

The powers of the various bodies which make secondary legislation and the way that legislation operates derive from the Treaties. If the Treaties are the primary source of community law then it does make logical sense to call the implementing rules secondary legislation; but it is essential to remember that secondary legislation is no less important or less powerful than primary legislation.

The three different types of secondary legislation are regulations, directives and decisions. We need to deal with each of them in turn.

Regulations

Article 189 of the Treaty of Rome states:

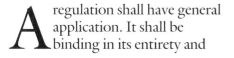

A regulation shall have general application. It shall be binding in its entirety and directly applicable in all member states.

This means that once a regulation is issued it immediately and automatically becomes part of the law of every member state. This is sometimes referred to as being 'directly applicable'. A member state does not need to pass an Act of Parliament, or equivalent, to make a regulation part of its domestic

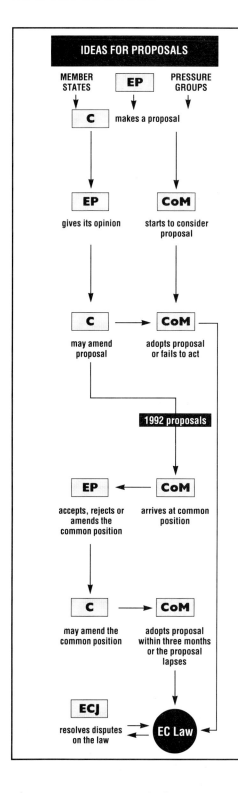

STAGE 1
Ideas for laws can come from the Commission (C), the European Parliament (EP), national governments, and sometimes pressure groups. Only the Commission can decide which ideas to turn into 'proposals' for future laws. The draft proposal is written by the appropriate Directorate General. The Commission may consult on a draft proposal, say, with national civil servants, businesses and consumer representatives.

STAGE 2
The Council of Ministers (CoM) starts to consider the formal proposal. Meanwhile, in the EP, it is examined by the appropriate Committee. An MEP is appointed to prepare a report on the proposal and steer the discussion of it at the committee stage. The Committee's view is then presented for debate by all MEPs during a session of Parliament. At the end of the debate, the EP votes on its opinion of the proposal which will be put to the Council of Ministers via the Commission. The opinion of the EP can be to accept, amend, or refuse to approve a proposal.

STAGE 3
The Commission can ignore the opinion of the EP, but more often than not, the Commission will redraft the original proposal to reflect some or all of the EP's amendments. Amended proposals which are not part of the single market programme are sent to the Council of Ministers who either fail to act or adopt the proposal, in which case it becomes law, either as a regulation or as a directive. Proposals which do come under the single market programme go on to Stage 4.

STAGE 4
1992 or single market proposals are amended (or not) in the light of the EP's opinion and then sent to the Council of Ministers. The Council is bound to reach a 'common position' which means that the 12 member states have arrived at a version of the proposal that all, or a majority of them, can eventually accept. The common position then goes back to the EP for debate within three months. The EP has to give its opinion on whether to accept the Council's common position or to amend or reject it by absolute majority.

STAGE 5
The EP's opinion on the common position goes back to the Commission. It has one month to decide whether to amend the common position accordingly. The proposal then goes back to the Council who have three months in which to reach a decision (though they can ask the EP for a one month extension). If the Council agrees to the Commission's amended proposal, it can be adopted by a majority vote. If the Council wants to stick by the original common position, the proposal must be adopted by a unanimous vote.

Figure 5.1 How Community law is made
Source: *Which?, June 1991*

law. A regulation is therefore a very powerful instrument of Community law-making, operating like a missile, bypassing the member state's own law-making process and penetrating the domestic law of that state.

Regulations may give individuals rights which can be enforced against other individuals and against member states.

Example:
Regulation 1390/81 has the effect of coordinating the social security schemes of member states so that a contribution made in one member state counts when a claim is made in a different member state.

This would give an individual claimant the right to enforce his claim in a domestic court where this was necessary.

Directives

Article 189 of the Treaty of Rome states:

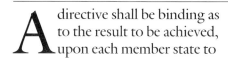 directive shall be binding as to the result to be achieved, upon each member state to which it is addressed, but shall leave to the national authorities the choice and form of methods.

Directives are initially issued in draft form for consultation purposes; but once they are agreed, member states are usually given a time limit within which to implement them.

How a member state implements a directive is a matter for that member state, as long as the desired result is obtained.

Example:
Directive 85/374 was implemented by the UK parliament in 1987 when it passed the Consumer Protection Act 1987 which imposes strict liability on the producers of defective products.

In the historic case of *Francovich and Bonifaci* v. *Italy*, the European Court of Justice ruled that the plaintiffs were entitled to compensation from their own government as a result of that government's failure to implement EC Directive 80/987 which provided for compensation to be paid following an employer's bankruptcy. And in *Marshall* v. *Southampton Area Health Authority* the Court held that a government could not, as employer, take advantage of its own failure to implement a Directive. *Francovich and Bonifaci* v. *Italy*. extends this principle out of the public sector and provides that governments may have to pay compensation to any citizen or undertaking who loses out as a result of inability to claim in a national court because of a non-implemented Directive.

These decisions will act as a powerful incentive to member states not to lag behind in the implementation of Directives; many cases have been brought since Francovich and Bonifaci, which will increase the rate at which member states implement Directives.

Decisions

Article 189 of the Treaty of Rome states:

decision shall be binding in its entirety upon those to whom it is addressed.

Decisions are likely to be issued in relation to an individual member state, individual or organization.

Example:
The Commission may decide, on application from an individual company, whether a cooperation agreement it has made with another company infringes Community competition law.

The European Court of Justice

The job of the European Court of Justice is to ensure that the rules of the Community are adhered to by individuals, member states and the other organizations of the Community. The Court decides what the relevant rules of Community law are and applies them where disputes arise between any of the bodies mentioned above.

A further task of the Court is to interpret the Treaties so that member states can ensure that decisions taken in national courts are taken in accordance with Community law. This is extremely important because:

- The Treaties create what amounts to a new body of law, one that is partly international because it binds states, and partly national because it also binds individuals and can be implemented in national courts. The final arbiter of what those rules are has to be a body which is supranational and has authority to ensure its decisions are adhered to.
- It would lead to chaos if the courts and governments of member states were to each interpret the Treaties in their own way, so that there were many different interpretations of the Treaties in existence at any one time. This point is further complicated by the fact that the Treaty of Rome exists in many member states only in translation and questions of interpretation are bound to arise.

Article 177

Article 177 of the Treaty of Rome gives the national courts of member states the power to refer cases to the European Court of Justice for a preliminary ruling on the meaning of any provision of the Treaty. The Court makes its interpretation and then refers it back to the national court, which proceeds to decide the case in accordance with the interpretation.

The European Court of Justice does not decide the case itself; it confines itself to deciding on the meaning of the relevant Treaty provision. The case is suspended while the Court's ruling is awaited.

If the question is a very serious one and the case ends up in the highest domestic court available, such as the House of Lords in the UK, then that court has a duty to refer the matter to the European Court of Justice, whose decision is binding on the domestic court; it *must* follow its interpretation.

British courts were initially reluctant to use this procedure, believing that their judges were capable of making decisions in accordance with Community law without the need for a referral. In recent years, however, it has been invoked much more frequently.

Example:

In *Torfaen Borough Council* v. *B & Q Plc* (145/88) the Article 177 procedure was invoked to establish whether or not UK Sunday trading laws contravened Article 30 of the Treaty of Rome. At that stage the Court decided that shop opening hours were possibly a restriction on trade which might be against Community law.

Unlike UK domestic courts, however, the European Court of Justice is not bound by any doctrine of precedent (i.e. it does not have to follow previous decisions). The House of Lords therefore decided to refer the matter to the European Court under Article 177 again and see if a different decision would be reached. The court reported in December 1992 that restricting Sunday opening involved no contravention of EC law.

A Summary

What, then, can we conclude at the end of this brief outline of Community law?

- That Community law takes priority over national law.
- That Community policies are implemented by secondary legislation.
- That some provisions of the Treaty of Rome are directly effective and can be claimed as rights by individuals in national courts.
- That parliamentary sovereignty has been limited by membership of the community.
- That where provisions of the Treaty need interpreting, the European Court of Justice may be called on, using the procedure outlined in Article 177.

A Final Note: The Possibility of Repeal

At the Edinburgh summit in 1992 the following declaration was adopted:

That some Community legislation be withdrawn on the grounds that they were not fully warranted in terms either of value added by Community actions or of comparative efficiency in relation to other possibilities of action in national or international courts.

It is not an acceptable reason for continuance of a provision, whatever it is, that the provision is enshrined in a separate convention if that convention does not give the right of action to an individual citizen.

The European Parliament of February 1993 comments on this proposal that it raises cause for concern that it could be the beginning of an attempt to dismantle EC legislation. However, the process of dismantling requires the agreement of the European Parliament, which will not allow repeal without the Commission presenting a well argued case.

part three

THE POLICIES OF THE EC

6

The single market

This chapter covers:
- a review of progress towards implementation of the 'four freedoms'
- policy on the free movement of labour
- policy on the free movement of goods
- competition policy

The 'Four Freedoms'

The objective of creating a single 'common market' among the Community member states was explicitly set out in Article 2 of the Treaty of Rome:

The Community shall have as its task by establishing a common market and progressively approximating the economic policies of member states, to promote throughout the Community a harmonious development of economic activities . . .

Also enshrined in the Treaty, in pursuit of the objective of the common market, were the so-called 'four freedoms' (see figure 6.1):

- the free movement of people
- the free movement of goods
- the free movement of services
- the free movement of capital

These were among the founding principles of the Community, on which its policies would be based.

The original six members of the Community had hoped to have implemented all the main aims of the founding Treaties within 12 years of their signature, and in particular by this time to have created a single European economy with common policies in key areas.

However, while progress was rapid in some areas, e.g. the Common Agricultural Policy (see chapter 8), it was very slow in others. Many of the original barriers to a single market remained, and new ones appeared. These included:

- the various obstacles to the free movement of people
- differing national technical specifications
- differing national health and safety standards
- differing national environmental regulations
- differing national quality controls

Together these restrictions on economic activity in the EC were known as non-tariff barriers, and they constituted a formidable obstacle to achievement of the single market.

Economic integration was also complicated by the addition of new members to the Community with widely differing degrees of economic development and a variety of established national practices.

The Single European Act and the Single Market

In contrast to the vision of the Community's founders, by the early 1980s a true common market was still a long way from reality. This was ironic, as in the minds of most people this was the Community's central purpose.

The Single European Act of 1986 established a tight timetable for the achievement of an open economic system in Europe in which the four freedoms would be a practical reality. It defined the single market as

---

An area without internal frontiers in which the free movement of goods, persons, services and capital is ensured in accordance with the provisions of the Treaty

---

and decreed that by 1 January 1993 all barriers to such a single market should be lifted.

In the intervening six years much work was done on the implications of the single market – and of failure to achieve it. In 1988 the Commission published *The European Challenge 1992: The Benefits of a Single Market* (popularly known as the Cecchini Report, after the chairman of the working party which produced it). This document estimated the costs to the industries of the Community of non-completion of the internal market and assessed the likely benefits of its achievement (see box).

THE COSTS OF NON-EUROPE
- high administrative costs incurred in dealing with different national bureaucratic requirements
- higher transport costs because of formalities at borders
- increased costs as a result of having to apply different national standards and so having smaller product runs
- duplication of costs involved in separate research and development
- high costs of non-competitive and heavily regulated state activities as exemplified by national public procurement policies
- high costs and reduced choice for consumers confined to their national markets
- the opportunity cost which prevents or discourages economic activity from spreading across frontiers to enjoy the full market potential

THE BENEFITS OF THE SINGLE MARKET
By 1988:

- a gain of about 4.5% (£129 billion) in Community GDP
- a reduction in prices of 6%
- the creation of 2 million extra jobs

Nevertheless, 1 January 1993 did not see the lifting of a curtain on a new market similar in operation to that existing among the states of the USA. Each of the four freedoms was at a different stage of development and progress towards a truly free market was likely to vary from one area to another.

PEOPLE

Border controls between some EC countries have vanished. Passport checks are lighter throughout the EC. New rules mean some qualifications are now recognized EC-wide, allowing people to work abroad more easily.

But: This is the area where most problems remain, and the EC has admitted that a border-free Europe does not yet exist. Britain is adamant some checks must remain, and Denmark, Greece and Ireland will also retain some controls. It will take until December 1993 to adapt airports to the new rules.

GOODS

Customs checks at borders between EC states have vanished; there is a new blue channel at customs, and millions of pages of customs forms have disappeared. Consumers can buy alcohol, tobacco and other products for personal use without restrictions on how much they can take home.

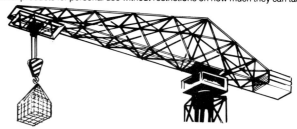

But: Prices continue to vary widely as VAT has not been equalized. New VAT payments and trade statistics are handled by an EC-wide system which some businesses believe is too complicated. It is still harder to buy imported cars in some EC states than in others.

SERVICES

Lawyers, engineers, accountants and teachers have been allowed to practise in other EC countries for more than a year. Opticians and some others will be able to practise in other countries in 1994. There will be a single banking licence and a similar scheme for insurance companies will be phased in.

But: In some areas, especially those connected with state ownership, such as telecommunications and broadcasting, there remain serious restrictions. In practice, there are still obstacles to selling other professional services across borders. Life insurance firms will have to wait until 1994 to operate freely in other EC countries.

CAPITAL

Citizens can borrow and save with EC banks which use their new freedom to do business outside their home state. Capital controls are lifted and business can invest freely throughout the EC.

But: Some special exemptions remain. Above all, there continue to be costs for changing money since the Single European Act does not establish a common currency. This is a key aim of the Maastricht treaty, yet to be ratified by Britain and Denmark.

Figure 6.1 The four freedoms: how the single market stood at the beginning of 1993

The remaining sections of this chapter will examine the Community's policy on the free movement of labour and goods.

Free movement of capital is dealt with in chapter 7 on Community monetary policy.

Free Movement of Labour

The rules about free movement of labour are contained in Articles 48–58 of the Treaty of Rome.

KEY PROVISIONS OF THE TREATY OF ROME

Article 48
- states that freedom of movement for workers shall be secured within the Community.
- abolishes discrimination based on nationality
- gives member states the rights to refuse entry to an applicant on the grounds that the personal conduct of an individual contravenes considerations of:
  - (a) public policy
  - (b) public security
  - (c) public health

Article 51
provides the right for nationals of a member state who are self-employed to establish themselves in business in the territory of another member state

Article 11 (Regulation 1612/68)
provides that the family of the national of a member state has the right to accompany a worker when he takes up employment or establishes himself in another member state. Family members do not have to be EC nationals. Cohabitees in a stable relationship are included in this right. Cohabitees in same-sex relationships are not

---

These provisions of the Treaty of Rome are supplemented by various regulations and directives and now by significant case law both in national courts and in the European Court of Justice.

Example: Van Duyn v. Home Office (Case 41/74) (1975) 2 WLR 760

In 1968 the UK government announced that it considered the Church of Scientology socially harmful in that it alienated families and damaged the psychological health of its followers. British immigration authorities refused to grant entry to Miss Van Duyn who had been given a job by the organization.

On Article 177 see
chapter 5

Miss Van Duyn claimed in an English court that the ban was unlawful because it was a breach of Article 48 of the Treaty of Rome. On a reference to the European Court of Justice under the Article 177 procedure the court confirmed the exclusion on the grounds that Miss Van Duyn's current connection with the Church of Scientology amounted to unacceptable personal conduct and that there was a genuine and serious threat to one of the fundamental interests of society. All of the four freedoms are subject to limitations which enable states, for example, to prevent the entry of persons where public policy, public health, or public security is at stake.

Free Movement of Goods

KEY PROVISIONS OF THE TREATY OF ROME

Article 9
The Community shall be based upon a customs union which shall cover all trade in goods, and which shall involve the prohibition between member states of customs duties on imports and exports and of all charges having equivalent effect and the adoption of a common customs tariff in their relation with third countries.

Article 30
Quantative restrictions on imports and all measures having equivalent effect shall . . . be prohibited between member states.

Article 95
No member state shall impose directly or indirectly on the products of other member states any internal taxation of any kind in excess of that imposed directly or indirectly on similar domestic products.

Example: Rewe-Zentral AG v. Bundesmonopolverwaltung fur Branntwein (Case 120/78)

(otherwise known as *Cassis de Dijon*)

Cassis is a blackcurrent liqueur produced in both France and Germany. That produced in France has an alcohol level of 15–20%. German regulations specified that spirits should have a 25% alcohol level. This meant that French cassis could not be marketed in Germany as it did not reach the minimum alcohol requirement.

Under the Article 177 procedure the European Court of Justice ruled that Article 30 of the Treaty of Rome had been breached by the German regulation. In reaching this decision the Court applied a test known as The Rule of Reason, which states that obstacles to free movement of goods which result from differences in national laws must go no further than is necessary to protect public health, consumers, commercial fairness or effective tax supervision. Any rules which in effect protect goods produced domestically against imported goods shall be in breach of Article 30.

The court also stated that goods which have been lawfully produced and marketed in one member state cannot be prevented from entering another member state and being marketed there unless the rule in the importing state which prohibits the importation and sale is deemed to be necessary to protect some legitimate interest.

This idea, that member states must recognize the legitimacy of a product lawfully marketed in another member state, was of great assistance in the development of the single European market. It establishes the principle of mutual recognition as a possible alternative to the harmonization of standards, a development which enabled the single market to be achieved more quickly than it otherise would have been.

Free Movement of Services

The rules about free movement of services are contained in Articles 59–66 of the Treaty of Rome.

KEY PROVISIONS OF THE TREATY OF ROME

Article 59
States that restrictions on freedom to provide services shall be abolished

Article 60
Defined services as *including*:
   (a)   activities of an industrial character
   (b)   activities of a commercial character
   (c)   activities of craftsmen
   (d)   activities of the professions
The wording of Article 60 here obviously means that provision of other services may also fall within the scope of the Article.

   Article 60 also provides that EC nationals who provide services in a member state shall be entitled to do so under the same conditions as nationals of that state.

continued . . .

> Article 1(1) (b) of Directive 73/148 also makes it clear that there shall be freedom for nationals of member states to go to another member state as a *recipient* of services. This would include, for example, tourists, students or persons seeking medical treatment.
>
> It is also important to note under the provision of services that Article 7 of the Treaty of Rome provides that 'any discrimination on the grounds of nationality shall be prohibited'.

Freedom to provide services has to be seen in the context of freedom of establishment, the essential difference between the two being that, according to Article 60, freedom to provide services means services of a *temporary* nature. Permanent provision of a service in another member state is part of the right of freedom of establishment.

On financial services in the Community, see chapter 7

Provision of financial services across the Community is not therefore established by Articles 59–60.

Competition Policy

Competition policy is a central component of the single market arrangements. In pursuit of the aim of preventing the erection of barriers to trade within the Community, it has three main objectives:

- To prevent companies from entering into price fixing and market sharing agreements.

> KEY PROVISIONS OF THE TREATY OF ROME
>
> **Article 85**
> The following shall be prohibited as incompatible with the common market: all agreements between undertakings, decisions by association of undertakings and concerted practices which may affect trade between member states and which have as their object *or effect* the prevention, restriction or distortion of competition within the common market.
>
> **Article 86**
> Any abuse by one or more undertakings of a dominant position within the common market or in a substantial part of it shall be prohibited as incompatible with the common market in so far as it may affect trade between member states.

- To prevent anti-competitive practices which may result from market power being concentrated into the hands of monopoly, duopoly or oligopoly.
- To prevent national governments from distorting competition in the community by favouring national companies.

Articles 85 and 86 of the Treaty of Rome contain a broad statement of Community policy on competition. These provisions are reinforced by regulations applied by the Commission and enforced by the European Court of Justice. Offending institutions can be ordered to terminate practices in contravention of Community rules and may be fined.

Example 1: Akzo Chemie BV v. Commission (1987) ICMLR 231

Akzo, a producer of chemicals, undercut the prices of ECS, a small British company that wished to expand into Akzo's market.

The Commission held that Akzo's actions were an abuse of its dominant position in the market and not only discouraged ECS from competing, but also deterred other companies from competing against Akzo in the future.

Example 2: Consten and Grundig v. Commission (1966) ECR 299

This case concerned an exclusive dealing agreement between Grundig, a manufacturer in Germany, and Consten, a distributor in France.

A condition of Consten's being Grundig's exclusive distributor in France was that Consten would not export to any other member states goods it had imported into France from Germany. The effect of this would be to restrict competititon in France and other member states. The European Court held that such an agreement was a breach of Article 85.

7
Economic and monetary policy

This chapter covers:
- Exchange rate policy in Europe in the 20th century
- The development of the European Monetary System
- The role of the Ecu
- The working of the Exchange Rate Mechanism
- The Delors Report on economic and monetary union
- The 'British protocol' on exemption from Stage Three
- The European Central Bank
- The problems of achieving economic convergence
- Financial services in the single market

Introduction: Exchange Rate Policy in Europe

An important pillar of the Single Market is the concept of monetary union. As long ago as the late 1960s it was recognized by the then member states of the Community that closer economic and monetary union was essential if the goals of the original Treaty of Rome were to be realized.

The European Community had no wish to repeat the economic mistakes of the inter-war period. During the 1920s and 1930s as world trade declined those countries who relied very heavily on overseas trade for their markets found themselves competing for a steadily diminishing market. Competitive devaluations became the order of the day as each country tried to obtain a price advantage over its trade rivals. Any gains achieved in this way were very short-term, as rival countries devalued in turn in order to re-establish the original price relationships.

During this period countries also used import quotas and tariffs to protect their own domestic goods from foreign competition. This protectionist approach, on top of the competitive devaluations, further decreased the level of foreign trade in real terms, thus only exacerbating the problem.

The Bretton Woods system: fixed exchange rates

Only rearmament and the coming of the Second World War in 1939 broke the cycle as countries' economies were revived with the demand for military goods and services. As the war seemed to be approaching its end, however, it was clear that new arrangements would have to be made to deal with the international economy. The Bretton Woods conference of 1944 established the International Monetary Fund (IMF) and a return to a system of fixed exchange rates, as had applied under the Gold Standard, which was abandoned in 1931. The IMF would ensure that member states maintained their respective exchange rates and that changes were agreed only if a member country had a persistent balance of payments surplus or deficit. Should a country's currency come under pressure in the foreign exchange market, that country could call on supplementary funds made available by the IMF to national central banks to support their currencies in such circumstances.

There are inherent difficulties in any fixed exchange rate scheme, and these soon became apparent. (To some extent they have been reflected in the recent operation of the EMS: see below.) Those countries with persistently high levels of inflation found this reflected in poor export performance and balance of payments deficits because their exports were relatively expensive on the world market. Conversely, those countries with low levels of inflation, such as Japan and Germany, found themselves with regular balance of payments surpluses because their exports were relatively cheap on the world market.

Countries that persistently operated a balance of payments deficit could not maintain a fixed rate of exchange for an indefinite period of time as they lacked the necessary gold and convertible foreign exchange reserves to maintain the par-value of their currency on the foreign exchange market. (Par-value was maintained by buying their own currency with gold and convertible foreign exchange reserves that were earned when the balance of payments was in surplus.)

If a country permanently operated a balance of payments surplus or deficit it was deemed to be in a state of 'fundamental disequilibrium' and speculators would therefore anticipate either a revaluation (balance of payment surplus) or devaluation (balance of payments deficit). In turn, the very buying or selling of the currency in question by speculators made it inevitable that an exchange rate change would indeed occur.

The Bretton Woods system of fixed exchange rates, unable to cope with the stresses that had developed, collapsed in 1971. It was replaced by a system of floating rates, in which each currency's value against others is determined by the interaction of supply and demand on the international currency markets. The IMF remained in being with a modified role, no longer underpinning a fixed-rate system.

From the Werner Report to the European Monetary System

In October 1970 at a summit held at the Hague, Community leaders made the first moves towards recognizing that the aims of the Treaty of Rome would not be met unless common or at least coordinated economic policies were brought into being. The leaders considered the report of a committee of financial and monetary experts, chaired by Luxembourg Prime Minister Pierre Werner. The Werner Report proposed:

- progressive unification of economic policies
- the estabishment of common monetary policies, embracing capital movements, tax harmonization and common budgetary policy, that would achieve, by 1980, a common EC currency and complete economic and monetary union.

Out of the Werner Repot emerged what was eventually to become the European Monetary System (EMS).

The EMS has two main objectives;

- to reduce exchange rate fluctuations between member state currencies
- to reduce the currency uncertainties involved with inter-member trade and thereby increase trade, economic growth and employment

'establishment by stages of economic and monetary union in the Community'.

One of the recommendations of the Werner Report was the establishment of the European Monetary Cooperation Fund (EMCF). This body was founded in 1973. As with the IMF and the Bretton Woods system, the EMCF plays an important role in the operation of the EMS and is seen by some as being an embryonic European Central Bank. The EMCF issues European Currency Units (Ecus) to the central banks of member states in exchange for gold and convertible currencies.

April 1972 saw the establishment of the European Community currency 'snake'. This was the forerunner of the present Exchange Rate Mechanism (ERM). Just like the ERM, its main role was to limit fluctuations in exchange rates between member state currencies. However, its success was limited: the UK's membership, for example, lasted only three months. By 1978 it was recognized that a more enduring system needed to be designed. In December 1978 agreement was reached on the EMS in the form in which it now exists. The EMS replaced the 'snake' in March 1979.

The EMS in operation

The advantages of membership

The European Monetary System is seen as an important mechanism for achieving the aim of European monetary union by 1999 (see below). Under the EMS, not only the currencies of member states are joined but also their economies.

Member states saw several related advantages in belonging to the ERM. The most important gains to members were seen to be:

- the movement towards low inflation
- the growth in trade between members resulting from lower levels of inflation
- economic growth and lower levels of unemployment resulting in turn from the growth in trade.

Governments also saw the EMS as an opportunity to create an area of monetary stability between the currencies of EC member states, especially important in view of the fact that inter-EC trade accounts for a significantly large proportion of many member states' exports.

So important was the EMS considered to be in underpinning the original objectives of the Treaty of Rome that it formed an integral part of the Single European Act of 1986 (see chapter 3). The role and importance of the EMS were further enhanced after 1 January 1993 when the single European market (SEM) came into full effect, which in turn put further pressure on moves towards full European Monetary Union.

Operational decisions concerning the EMS are the result of collective agreement between member state central banks and their respective Finance Ministers. Each of these two groups meets regularly; the Central Banks through the EC Governors' Committee in Basle and the finance ministers through ECOFIN (European Council of Finance Ministers) in Brussels.

How the Exchange Rate Mechanism works

Each member state's currency entered the ERM at an agreed exchange rate against the Ecu. All the member states' currencies are weighted against it according to their various strengths.

The exchange at which a member state's currency enters the ERM is set by the governors of the other member states' central banks and their respective finance ministers. As the German Deutschmark was the strongest of all the EC currencies in terms of low inflation and interest rates, some member states who joined the ERM additionally 'pegged' their currencies to the Deutschmark.

Britain joined the ERM in October 1990, at the same time as the Spanish peseta; sterling was pegged to the Deutschmark at a rate of DM2.95 to the pound. A condition of entry for both Britain and Spain was that their respective currencies were allowed a float of plus or minus 6% either side of the agreed entry rate. Other member countries operate a plus or minus fluctuation of 2.25%, a figure which both Britain and Spain will eventually have to achieve if they wish to participate in complete monetary union before the planned adoption by January 1999 of the Ecu as a common currency.

What is the Ecu?
- the denominator of the ERM
- the unit of account for the intervention mechanisms of the ERM
- a measure of the divergence of currencies from their central rates within the EMS
- the reserve instrument for member states' central banks and the unit of exchange of inter-bank settlements between member states
- from 1999 (under present plans) the common European currency

---

THE COMPOSITION OF THE ECU

The Ecu (European Currency Unit) is a basket of EC currencies, composed of specific amounts of each currency in proportion to the economic strengths of the EC members. The amounts were last revised in September 1989 when the Spanish peseta and Portuguese escudo joined the basket. While the amounts remain unchanged, the relative weights fluctuate, as do the EMS currencies against each other. In addition to the official Ecu used in the EMS there is also a private Ecu which is increasingly being used for banking and investment, particularly in the Eurobond market in which there are now over 70 billion Ecu of bonds outstanding.

0.6242
Deutschmark
30.48%

6.885
Peseta
5.36%

1.332
French Franc
19.09%

0.2198
Netherlands
Florin
9.52%

50
Ecu

0.08784
£
12.48%

3.431
Belgian Franc
8.13%

1.04741
Escudo
0.79%

0.008552
Irish punt
1.12%

1.44
Drachma
0.63%

0.1976
Danish Krone
2.5%

151.8
Lira
9.90%

EXCHANGE RATES TO THE ECU As at Sept 16 1991	
Belgium and Luxembourg franc	42.33
Danish krone	7.917
German Deutschmark	2.051
Greek drachma	227.49
French franc	6.985
Dutch guilder	2.312
Irish punt	0.767
Italian lira	1535.00
Portuguese escudo	175.95
Spanish peseta	128.59
UK pound sterling	0.703

KEY TO FIGURES

0.6242	amount
Deutschmark	currency
30.48%	relative weight

Figure 7.1 The composition of the Ecu, showing relative weights and exchange rates of component currencies at 16 September 1991

Table 7.1 Exchange Rate Mechanism: Bilateral central rates and intervention points (from 6 April 1992)*

		UK£	BFr/LuxFr	FFr	L	FI	DM	DK	IR£	Pta	Esc
£1 United Kingdom	+6%		64.6050	10.5055	2343.62	3.52950	3.13200	11.9479	1.16920	203.600	272.320
	central rate		60.8451	9.89389	2207.25	3.32389	2.95000	11.2526	1.10118	191.750	256.470
	-6%		57.3035	9.31800	2078.79	3.13050	2.77800	10.5976	1.03710	180.590	241.545
100 BFr/LuxFr Belgium/Luxembourg	+2.25%	1.74510		16.6310	3710.20	5.58700	4.95900	18.9143	1.85100	334.619	447.560
	central rate	1.64352		16.2608	3627.64	5.46286	4.84837	19.4938	1.80981	315.143	421.513
	-2.25%	1.54790		15.8990	3546.90	5.34150	4.74000	18.0831	1.76950	296.802	396.980
100 Ffr France	+2.25%	10.7320	628.970		22817.0	34.3600	30.4950	116.320	11.3830	2057.80	2752.40
	central rate	10.1073	614.977		22309.1	33.5953	29.8164	113.732	11.1299	1938.06	2592.21
	-2.25%	9.5190	601.295		21813.0	32.8475	29.1500	111.200	10.8825	1825.30	2441.30
1000 L Italy	+2.25%	0.481050	28.1930	4.58440		1.54000	1.36700	5.21400	0.510246	92.2400	123.380
	central rate	0.435053	27.5661	4.48247		1.50590	1.33651	5.09803	0.498895	86.8726	116.194
	-2.25%	0.426690	26.9530	4.38300		1.47250	1.30650	4.98500	0.487799	81.8200	109.430
100 Dfl Netherlands	+2.25%	31.9450	1872.15	304.440	67912.0		90.7700	346.240	33.8868	6125.30	8190.00
	central rate	30.0853	1830.54	297.661	66405.3		88.7526	338.537	33.1293	5768.83	7715.97
	-2.25%	28.3340	1789.85	291.040	64928.0		86.7800	331.020	32.3939	5433.10	7267.00
100 DM Germany	+2.25%	35.9970	2109.50	343.050	76540.0	115.235		390.160	38.1825	6901.70	9233.60
	central rate	33.8984	2062.55	335.386	74821.7	112.673		381.443	37.3281	6500.00	8693.93
	-2.25%	31.9280	2016.55	327.920	73157.0	110.1675		373.000	36.4964	6121.70	8190.00
100 DKr Denmark	+2.25%	9.43610	553.000	89.9250	20062.0	30.2100	26.8100		10.0087	1809.40	2420.10
	central rate	8.88687	540.723	87.9257	1965.4	29.5389	26.2162		9.78604	1704.05	2279.22
	-2.25%	8.36970	528.700	85.9700	19179.0	28.8825	25.6300		9.56830	1604.90	2146.60
1 IR£ Ireland	+2.25%	0.964240	56.5115	9.18900	2050.03	3.08700	2.74000	10.4511		184.892	247.299
	central rate	0.908116	55.2545	8.98480	2004.43	3.01848	2.67894	10.2186		174.131	232.905
	-2.25%	0.855260	54.0250	8.78500	1959.84	2.95100	2.61900	9.9913		163.997	219.350
100 Pta Spain	+6%	0.553740	33.6930	5.47850	1222.30	1.84050	1.63300	6.23100	0.609772		142.020
	central rate	0.521514	31.7316	5.15981	1151.11	1.73345	1.53847	5.86837	0.574281		133.753
	-6%	0.491160	29.8850	4.85950	1084.10	1.63250	1.44900	5.52600	0.540858		125.970
100 Esc Portugal	+6%	0.414000	25.1900	4.09610	913.800	1.37600	1.22100	4.65860	0.455895	79.3850	
	central rate	0.389909	23.7241	3.85772	860.626	1.29601	1.15023	4.38747	0.429360	74.7649	
	-6%	0.367220	22.3435	3.63320	810.500	1.22100	1.08300	4.13210	0.404371	70.4130	

*The table shows the amount of the currency in the left-hand column. In each cell the central rate and the upper and the lower limits are given. Thus, for example, the central rate between sterling and the lira is 2207.25 lire per pound (or £0.453053 per L 1,000). *Source:* Bank of England

Table 7.1 illustrates the bilateral central rates and intervention points as of April 1992. 'Intervention points' are the upper and lower limits of each country's exchange rates beyond which the central bank of that country must intervene to restore it to the agreed band. For example, a member country's currency may come under pressure in the foreign exchange markets due to a large balance of payments deficit or high levels of inflation in comparison to other member states. This pressure may be forcing the currency to the floor of its 2.25% float (6% in the case of the UK and Spain). In this case the central bank would be required to buy its currency in the foreign exchange market using its reserves of convertible currencies (e.g. dollar, yen, franc); if the currency were approaching the upper limit, it would be required to sell. Should support be required on a larger scale, central banks of other member states may be asked to participate in either buying or selling as appropriate.

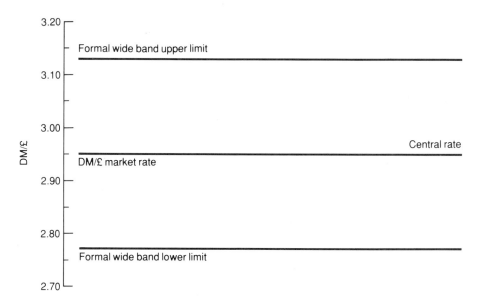

Figure 7.2 The sterling/Deutschmark exchange rate band
Source: *Bank of England*

The EMS has in addition created specific credit systems to which member states' central banks have access and which can be called upon for intervention purposes. These sytems are known as VSTF or 'very short-term financing' facilities. Credit is available for a three-month period, after which it must normally be repaid, though it is possible for some of the borrowings to be carried forward for another three months. After this second period there can be no subsequent extension. VSTF is available only when it is necessary to finance 'obligatory intervention'; that is, when the currency in question is at the margins of its permissible range. VSTF finance operates via the EMCF.

There have been twelve realignments since the EMS started, but most were in the early years, and recently the system has been stable.

	Date	Currency	% Realignment*
1979	13 March: Start of the EMS		
	24 September	DM	+2
		DK	−2.9
	3 December	DK	−4.76
1981	23 March	L	−6
	5 October	DM, Fl	+5.5
		FFr, L	−3
1982	22 February	BFr	−8.5
		DK	−3
	14 June	DM, Fl	+4.25
		L	−2.75
		FFr	−5.75
1983	22 March	DM	+5.5
		Fl	+3.3
		DK	+2.5
		BFr	+1.5
		FFr, L	−2.5
		IR£	−3.5
1985	22 July	BFr, DK, DM, FFr, IR£, Fl	+2
		l	−6
1986	7 April	DM, Fl	+3
		BFr	+1
		DK	+1
		FFr	−3
	4 August	IR£	−8
1987	12 January	DM, Fl	+3
		BFr	+2
1989	19 June	Entry of Spanish peseta	
1990	8 January	L (adoption of narrow band)	−3.7
1990	8 October	Entry of pound sterling	
1992	6 April	Entry of Portuguese escudo	

*The net charge in a particular central rate is approximately equal to the difference in the percentage changes shown against the two currencies concerned. For example, in March 1983 the Deutschmark was revalued by 2% against the guilder and 9% against the Irish punt.

Figure 7.3 Chronology of central rate changes within the EC
Source: *Bank of England*

In addition, or as an alternative to these options within the EMS, the government whose currency is under pressure may resort to domestic monetary policy controls; in particular, changes in interest rates.

In the event of either or both of these approaches failing, the member state faces two policy alternatives:

- First, it may seek approval for a realignment of its exchange rate *vis-à-vis* other member currencies away from its ERM entry rate. If there are upward pressures forcing the exchange rate towards the top of the band it can revalue, if it is at the bottom it can devalue. An individual member state cannot unilaterally decide to realign its currency; agreement must be reached with all other EMS states. In order to avoid currency speculation such meetings and announcements are formally made at the weekend at a time when the foreign exchange markets are closed.

- Secondly, and more drastically, it can temporarily leave the ERM. This option was taken by the UK government in September 1992, when the costs of supporting the pound (estimated at £1.8 billion), and temporary increases in interest rates to 15% were ineffective in reversing the decline of the pound's value against other EC currencies. The British government and the Bank of England realized that there was no alternative to letting sterling find its own level on the foreign exchange markets. January 1993 likewise saw Irish shot-term overnight interest rates rise from 50% to 100%, forcing the government to devalue the punt.

The European Exchange Rate Mechanism is recognized as being far from perfect. It is a halfway house between a fixed and a floating exchange rate system and is consequently vulnerable to speculative attacks. An obvious problem for the UK government, business organizations and individuals alike is that the UK economy has not been able to spend its way out of the current recession, for such action would probably have forced the pound towards the lower end of its band.

A fundamental problem facing all parties to the existing ERM is that there is no mechanism to share out amongst members the costs of defending a currency which comes under pressure; at present the task falls solely upon the central bank of the country involved.

It is for these reasons that the EC is striving, via the Maastricht Treaty, to achieve total European monetary union with a European Central Bank and one common European currency, the Ecu, by 1999.

European Monetary Union

The Delors Report

In 1988 the Delors Committee was established, with the task of proposing stages by which economic and monetary union (EMU) might be achieved. EMU was to be based on strict economic principles that would have to be observed by member states. Members could be part of this union only if they could prove that they had achieved stated standards of economic performance.

In 1989 the Delors Committee published its Report. It set out three stages by which EMU is to be arrived at.

Stage One

Stage One is centred on working towards the ratification by all member states of the Maastricht Treaty. The Maastricht Treaty is crucial to any further progress with EMU, for it created 'new' EC institutions that would achieve the objects of Stages Two and Three. During this stage, launched under EC powers already in existence, member states are to work more closely together in integrating their economic and monetary policies. Once the Maastricht Treaty has been ratified by all member states, Stage Two commences. The current date for the start of Stage Two is 1 January 1994.

Stage Two

The second stage involves the further harmonization of policies regarding interest rates, exchange rates and monetary policy in preparation for the transition to the final stage, Stage Three. From the beginning of 1994, signatories to the Maastricht Treaty will be expected to initiate the processes that lead to the eventual independence of their national central banks from government control and influence.

EMU: THE DELORS REPORT (1989)

Stage 1:
from 1 July 1990

Stage 2:
from 1 January 1994

Stage 3:

Establishment by 1 January 1993 of a single European market in:

- free movement of goods, services, labour and capital
- linkage of member states' currencies via the European Monetary System (EMS)

Establishment of Exchange Rate Mechanism (ERM) to which all member states belong

Currency fluctuations to be ±2.25% against the Ecu and each other

Movement towards the harmonization of:

- interest rates
- exchange rates
- monetary policies
- closer currency
- fluctuation bands

Establishment by 1 January 1994 of European Monetary Institute (EMI), fore-runner of European Central Bank (ECB)

Process leading to the eventual independence of member state central banks from government control to begin

European System of Central Banks established by July 1988, superseding the EMI

Member countries' exchange rates fixed permanently. Establishment of a single European currency, the Ecu, by 1 January 1999

Establishment of Common Monetary Policy

Establishment of a European Central Bank to:

- define and implement Community monetary policy
- conduct foreign exchange operations
- hold and manage official foreign exchange reserves of member states

---

EMU: The Essential Requirements

1994 Establishment of European Monetary Institute as forerunner of European Central Bank

1996 Finance ministers to assess which members satisfy stated convergence criteria:

- *Inflation*   Applicant to have level of inflation no more than 1.5% above the average of the lowest three inflation rates among all member states
- *Interest rates*   Applicant to have rates that are within 2% of the average of the lowest three rates among all member states
- *Debts*   Public sector debt must not exceed 60% of the applicant's GDP
- *Devaluation/revaluation*   Applicant's national currency not to have been devalued in the two-year period prior to application. Currency to have remained within 2.25% of margin of fluctuation allowed by ERM during this two-year period

1996 EC to initiate moves towards a single currency

July 1988 European Council to agree that a minimum of seven member states satisfy or are 'working towards' satisfying these criteria

January 1999 Adoption by countries approved at that summit of the Ecu as their common currency (Britain excepted)

Also during 1994 the European Monetary Institute is to be established as the forerunner of the European Central Bank, which will come into operation under Stage Three.

Stage Three

The final stage may occur in 1997 if sufficient member states have successfully met, though Stage 2, the necessary convergence criteria (see box). The European Commission and the European Monetary Institution (EMI) will advise the European Council by December 1996 whether a majority of signatories meet the agreed five stipulations.

According to the terms of the Maastricht Treaty, if by 31 December 1997 no decision has been taken on progress to Stage Three, a meeting of the European Council will be held in July 1998. If this summit agrees that at least seven member states satisfy or are 'working towards' satisfying the convergence criteria, the European System of Central Banks will be established and Stage 3 will come into effect on 1 January 1999. The European Council will determine by qualified majority voting (see chapter 4) which member states join Stage 3.

Stage 3 will see the adoption of a common EC monetary policy and establishment of a European Central Bank working with the European System of Central Banks. The currencies of the member states will be fixed permanently in relation to each other and for those that meet the convergence criteria will be replaced by a single common European currency, the Ecu. The Ecu will be a currency in its own right.

However, even when EMU is achieved member countries and firms will not be able to ignore currency fluctuations altogether, having to take into account the exchange rate of the European Ecu with other international currencies and trading blocks.

The 'British protocol'

Under the terms of the Maastricht Treaty, Britain has the right to opt out from the single currency and full economic convergence. This 'opt-out' facility was obtained by a special protocol in the Treaty which states that the UK government is not committed to move with the other signatories to Stage Three of EMU from January 1997. Any such commitment in the future would require the specific approval of the British parliament.

The British protocol
- UK government to retain its existing powers over both monetary policy and exchange rate policy
- The existing 'weighted votes' of the UK government suspended in terms of calculating qualified majority voting on EMU decisions
- The UK to have no voice in the appointment of officials to the executive board of the proposed European Central Bank
- European Central Bank policies not to apply to UK
- References by the Council of the European Central Bank to member state central banks to exclude Bank of England

---

The European Central Bank and ECOFIN

The European Central Bank (ECB) will grow out of the European Monetary Institute (EMI) which, if all goes according to the plan set out in the Delors Report, will be established in 1994. Once the ECB is established (planned to occur in 1999) member states' existing central banks will, like the present German Bundesbank, have to be independent of control by their respective governments. It is intended that the ECB will take the current German Bundesbank as its model: for example, one of its main policy objectives will be obtaining price stability throughout member states, as the Bundesbank does for Germany at present.

Membership of the ECB Council will consist of national central bank governors, who will hold their seats for a minimum of five years. Council members will be independent and will be required to ignore domestic economic and political considerations when considering ECB policies. The Bank will also have an Executive Board of six members, appointed by the European Council, who will sit for a period of eight years. The European Commission President can participate in the ECB Council but has no voting rights.

The European Parliament will receive annual reports from the ECB and will have the power to question the ECB President. It has the right to be both informed and consulted on aspects of EC monetary policy.

The European Council of Finance Ministers (ECOFIN) will, in consultation with the ECB, decide EC exchange rate policy. Once complete monetary union has been achieved the European Commission will monitor member governments' budgets.

The ECB will, if it feels appropriate, via ECOFIN:

- issue warnings and/or recommend policy changes
- cut any credits that member states may be receiving from the European Investment Bank
- require member states to hand over a proportion of their non-interest bearing deposits
- suspend EC regional aid
- impose fines

ECOFIN will also have the role of issuing broad economic guidelines in order to ensure that the European Community as a whole keeps to its stated economic objectives. If it feels that any individual member state is out of step and is following policies that it considers to be inconsistent with EMU then it will have the power to issue 'recommendations' as to more appropriate policies.

Convergence: some issues and problems

An important precondition for adherence to the agreed timetable for full EMU is 'economic convergence' among member states in the areas of inflation, interest rates, budget deficits and public debt. This is an ambitious programme and progress has been uneven. As the EC moves towards Stage Two of EMU the majority of member states are not on target in terms of working towards EMU convergence criteria. Only Luxembourg currently meets all the agreed criteria, while Greece and Portugal do not yet meet any.

	INFLATION		BOND YIELD		DEFICIT RATIO		DEBT RATIO		ERM
	LATEST	1992f	LATEST	1992f	LATEST	1992f	LATEST	1992f	
Germany	3.3	4.0	8.1	8.0	2.9	3.4	42.0	43.5	✓
France	3.0	3.0	9.0	8.4	2.1	2.3	47.4	48.5	✓
Netherlands	4.0	3.8	8.4	8.3	2.7	3.4	78.9	79.9	✓
UK	4.8	4.9	9.3	9.4	1.7	4.6	35.4	38.5	✗
Spain	6.2	6.3	12.6	11.5	4.4	4.9	45.8	48.0	✗
Italy	5.5	5.6	14.0	14.1	10.2	11.3	102.9	107.8	✓
Belgium	2.6	3.2	9.0	8.7	6.0	5.5	131.9	132.9	✓
Denmark	2.5	2.5	9.3	9.0	2.0	2.1	60.7	61.6	✓
Greece	15.8	15.0	19.2	19.0	17.1	14.5	84.1	87.1	✗
Portugal	9.5	9.0	13.2	13.0	5.4	4.5	64.7	62.7	✗
Ireland	3.6	3.6	9.3	8.9	1.9	1.9	113.3	108.8	✓
Luxembourg	3.6	3.2	8.2	8.2	−1.9	−2.0	6.9	6.5	✓
TARGET	**4.2**	**4.3**	**11.1**	**10.7**	< 3.0	< 3.0	< 60.0	< 60.0	

Figure 7.4 EMU convergence criteria: how the member states are progressing
Source: *The European*

The costs of convergence

The political and economic costs of meeting these targets are considerable
and in many cases may be unacceptable. In the UK, for example, further
action would be required to reduce an increasing budget deficit and
increasing levels of public debt at a time when the country is suffering from
the worst recession for over 50 years, with over 60,000 business
bankruptcies in 1992 and the level of unemployment set to go beyond 10%
in 1993. During Britain's membership of the ERM the Chancellor of the
Exchequer had to rely unduly heavily on the monetary policy tool of
interest rates in order to keep sterling within its agreed band. In
consequence the domestic UK economy may have suffered a deeper and
longer recession than would have been the case had the UK not joined the
ERM when it did.

Britain is not alone in the policy dilemma it faces. If countries such as
Italy adopted similar policies at a time when the German economy is
slowing down the whole of the EC could face prolonged recession.

In 1992 the German Bundesbank raised domestic interest rates in order to slow down inflation. The result has been a drop in German GDP which in turn is resulting in lower imports into Germany of goods from other EC member states with a consequent impact on their economies. An IMF report stated in 1992 that the economic measures that will be necessary in order to guarantee the meeting of the convergence criteria will result in a drop in economic growth across the EC of between 0.4% and 0.8% per year between 1993 and 1996, a development which could raise unemployment levels throughout the EC to 18–19 million by 1996. This projection has serious political implications for member states.

The national policy options

Membership of the ERM has made realignment (either devaluation or revaluation) of a member state's currency difficult, with the result that apart from a limited range of monetary policies – mainly interest rate changes – member states have few policy choices in addressing the difficult task of trying to make their economies more efficient. Table 7.2 illustrates the options being taken in 1992. Figure 7.5 shows the relative success of countries' attempts to limit inflation.

Table 7.2 Policies adopted by member states in pursuit of economic convergence (1992)

Country	Policy
Belgium	spending cuts
France	Spending cuts
Germany	VAT rise
Netherlands	Fiscal restructuring
Spain	Tightest budget for 10 years
UK	Painful cap on spending in a time of recession

Source: SG Warburg, *Financial Times* 28 October 1992

'Delors 2' and the EC Cohesion Fund

The idea of the Cohesion Fund arose during the Maastricht summit. The Fund, intended to be in operation by the end of 1993, would provide financial assistance for the poorer member states of the Community – Greece, Ireland, Portugal and Spain. The assistance would be granted for

- the estabishment within these states of appropriate parts of a trans-European energy, communications and transport network
- environmental improvement schemes.

The political impetus behind the Fund proposal was the need to win backing from these poorer states for the goal of economic and monetary union by 1999. Only by offering some financial incentive could their support be assured.

The Fund was intended to be financed by the so-called 'Delors 2' package, suggested by the Commission President in early 1992. This would involve member states increasing their total financial contributions to the EC budget from the 1992 level of 66.5 billion Ecu to 86.2 billion Ecu by 1999.

The European Monetary System: A Review of Impacts and Prospects

There is much debate on the economic and political issues associated with the EMS. Some believe that the single European market will be badly flawed if it is not complemented by a single European currency, the Ecu. Some member states are concerned at the dominance of the German economy and of the Deutschmark; this economic strength, they argue, is reflected in the political influence that Germany has over the general direction of EC policies, especially on the economic front.

The dominance of the Deutschmark

Throughout the existence of the EMS German inflation rates have been the lowest of all EC members. Because of this it has been very difficult for countries to realign their currencies, usually downwards, as a result of their higher levels of inflation. The pressures of ERM membership have meant that in practice countries have had to put aside the domestic pain created as they adopted policies that would ensure maintenance of their currency within the agreed bands.

Another consequence of the continued dominance of the German economy and the strength of the Deutschmark is that member states have set the central rates of their currencies against the Deutschmark rather than the Ecu, and it is the rate against the Deutschmark that has tended to inform opinion as to how well or badly that economy is performing.

In economic – and, to some extent political – terms, the German Bundesbank is seen to dominate the operation of the EMS and not to operate as an equal partner with the other EC central banks. This feeling was reflected in the debate that followed the UK's temporary withdrawal from the ERM in September 1992, when some observers claimed that the Bundesbank did not wish to support sterling.

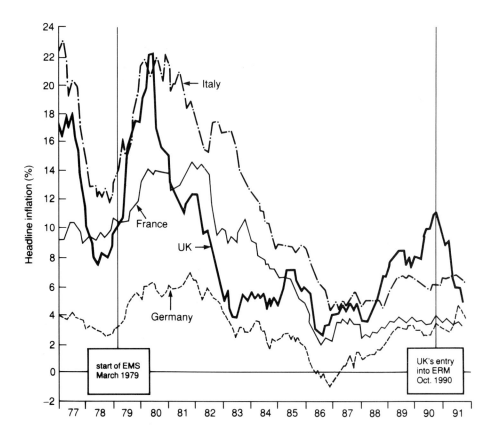

Figure 7.5 The EMS and economic convergence: the inflation example
Source: *Datastream*

One of the economic arguments in support of EMU is that it will help to remove any perceived economic and/or political influence by any other member state. Once the policy objective of convergence is achieved in terms of inflation rates, economic growth and interest rates, then the dominance of the Bundesbank will decline. Moreover, 1993/4 is likely to see the German economy stand still, with zero GDP growth; this will also weaken its influence.

Does the EMS have a distorting effect?

Some commentators on the EMS and ERM have expressed the view that the bands within which currency fluctuations are allowed unduly hinder countries from applying a wider variety of monetary policies. It can also be argued that the policies currently adopted by members to ensure that their currencies stay within the bands can have the effect of disguising major structural problems within national economies. For example, prior to withdrawal from the ERM in 1993 the UK had to maintain the value of sterling within the agreed bands of fluctuation as a point of principle.

This was seen as evidence of their underlying commitment to monetary union and a single currency by 1999. In order to maintain the value of the pound, the government placed great emphasis on bringing the rate of inflation in the UK down to that of Germany. This they did by adopting a high level of interest rates which in turn had the effect of deflating the economy, with severe consequences for business activity, employment etc. Membership of the ERM and a strong anti-inflationary policy were sold as being dependent on each other. As events after September 1992 have illustrated, what the UK economy in fact needed was low levels of interest rates and a devalued currency.

The benefits of the EMS

The EMS has brought some benefits. There is little doubt that it has been responsible for reducing the level of currency fluctuations, which in turn has assisted the growth of trade both within the EC and with the rest of the world. However, regarding inter-EC trade the currency conversion costs for small to medium-sized companies remain one of the biggest obstacles to cross-border EC trade; these will be removed with EMU. The present lack

---

SIGNPOSTS TO ECONOMIC AND MONETARY INTEGRATION

1957	Treaty of Rome establishes the EEC
1962	Concept of economic and monetary union debated by the European Commission
1970	Werner Report advocated economic and monetary union
1979	European Monetary System (EMS) established. The Ecu is created
1986	Single European Act establishes the goal of free movement of goods, services, labour and capital, to be effected by 1 January 1993
1990	Britain joins EMU (October)
1991	Treaty on European Union (Maastricht) agreed. Firm commitment by member states to EMU by 1 January 1999 at the latest; 1997 favoured
1992	Britain and Spain 'temporarily' leave the ERM
1994	Stage Two of EMU. Establishment of European Monetary Institute (EMI). EMI to draw up the necessary provisions for Stage Three
1997/1999	Stage Three of EMU. Conversion of those EC country currencies that meet convergence criteria to the Ecu. EMI becomes European Central Bank.

of a common currency also restricts the free movement of labour and capital within the EC, the two other key factors required for a true single market.

Furthermore, in bearing heavily on inflation the EMS has forced upon some governments an element of financial discipline in the conduct of their business. Membership of the EMS/ERM is also seen by the rest of the world, and the foreign exchange markets in particular, as a commitment to the underlying principles of the original Treaty of Rome and the single European market.

Towards Stage Three

In terms of meeting the timetable for EMU and a single currency there is still much to be done in achieving significant convergence not just of European currencies but also of the economies involved. On current projections, it seems unlikely that the preconditions for monetary union will be met within the period defined in the Delors Report.

It is now recognized that there may be significant costs involved in the run-up to EMU, which is planned for 1997 but is in practice not likely to occur before 1999. As member states approach 1997 and 1999 they will be faced with the necessity of complying with Maastricht Treaty convergence criteria. Some countries, such as Italy, may well be faced with the choice between either engineering a short-term fall in GDP by policies to lower inflation, or not joining EMU.

The European Commission's own research (published in October 1990 in the report *One Market, One Money*) accepts that there will be short-term costs in terms of the policies necessary to cut inflation and budget deficits. However, the long-term gains, especially those resulting from lower interest rates, will bring benefits to the whole Community.

Financial Services in the Single Market

Countries impose a number of restrictions on financial services activities across their borders, for a wide variety of reasons, including:

- to enable them to charge and collect tax
- to promote particular social and economic policies or other objectives.

These restrictions have the effect of distorting to a greater or lesser degree the way in which financial markets operate. This in turn involves costs both to the individual and to the organization.

The importance of financial services within the single market and the need for firms to have the right to obtain and trade in financial services freely throughout the EC have grown over the last 10–15 years. Apart from the desire to allow market forces to operate in the provision of financial services, the pressure to extend the single market to financial services was further intensified by the growth and application of new technology in all the major financial centres of the world, thereby enabling cross-border transactions on a hugely expanded scale and intensifying global financial competition.

Developments in banking and insurance

Within the EC there is a growing trend for bank mergers and an increasing interest by these enlarged banks in areas of activity outside the traditional range of banking, in particular insurance. With the establishment of the single European market from 1993 it is likely that an increasing number of the established insurance companies will be actively seeking links with the new 'Euro banks' especially in order to exploit new geographical areas of activity.

Northern Europe is seen as being 'well-covered' in that both individuals and business organisations accept and utilise a wide variety of insurance services. On the other hand Southern Europe, eg Italy and Greece, are seen as areas for considerable growth.

Currency transactions: costs and benefits

One of the consequences of European monetary union on the existing financial services sector will be a sharp decline in the European market for 'futures'.

As a generalization, contracts for the delivery of goods are of two types – 'spot' and 'forward'. In the case of 'spot' the person/organization purchasing the goods will be expected to pay the contract price either when the goods are delivered or when the relevant contract papers are received. The 'spot' price is the market price prevailing at the time of agreement. Under 'forward' or 'futures' contracts the contracted price does not have to be paid until an agreed specified date in the future. The goods in question may or may not have been delivered by that date.

'Forward' or 'future' prices are an agreed estimate as to what the prevailing 'spot' or market price will be at the time of delivery. This price is arrived at by taking into account such predictions as anticipated demand and supply conditions, rates of inflation, etc. The predicted 'future' market price may be higher or lower than that ruling at the time the original contract was made. If the spot price at the future date proves to be below the agreed price the seller would make a profit, if above the buyer would gain.

These transactions may be further complicated if the contract is to be paid for in a foreign currency. Forward exchange rates apply, whereby a seller can agree a forward exchange rate that will be applied to the transaction in question. These rates are quoted by foreign exchange dealers.

Forward exchange rates reduce the risks of sellers' income being unduly influenced by changes in market exchange rates.

At present some 57% of UK exports by value are with other European Community member states. The currency pressures of September 1992 resulting in the temporary withdrawal of the UK from the ERM underline the need for those companies involved in importing and exporting within the EC to protect themselves from fluctuations in the value of the contract currency between the time of signing a contract and its completion. Economic and monetary union, with the planned introduction by January 1999 of a single European currency, the Ecu, will remove this need and reduce the currency costs involved in intra-EC trade, currently estimated to be in the order of 6.2 billion to 10.4 billion Ecu.

The need for travellers between member states to convert currencies every time they cross a border will also be history by 1999 if EMU is achieved. There will thus be a benefit to the individual in terms of having more money to spend; but there will also be a loss to the financial services sector in terms of the profits currently made in commission on currency conversion. The Cecchini Report (see chapter 6) estimated that the establishment of a free market in financial services within the EC would itself bring cost benefits to organizations in excess of 20 billion Ecu.

The European Economic Area

In October 1991 agreement was reached between the EC and the European Free Trade Association (EFTA) to establish the EEA (European Economic Area). The EEA will join the existing EFTA countries (Austria, Finland, Iceland, Norway, Sweden, Switzerland) with the 12 EC countries to form an enlarged common market population of 380 million. This will in itself provide further impetus towards the establishment of a uniform and harmonized system for financial services as members of EFTA bring their existing financial services regulations into line with those that are being harmonized within the EC.

The impact of Directive 85/611

From 1 January 1993 firms have the right to trade financial services throughout the Community on the basis of a 'single authorization passport' from their home member state. It is anticipated that by the end of 1993 there will be a place home country authorization in banking, investment services and non-life insurance.

The concept of a 'single authorization passport' is set down in EC Directive 85/611 on 'Undertakings for Collective Investments in Transferable Securities' (UCITS), which states that once a UCITS has received the necessary approval in its home member country then it can, subject to any regulations existing in other member states, with respect to, e.g., marketing, be sold in those states. This Directive is instrumental in assisting the EC to achieve its goal of the free movement of capital as laid down in the original Treaty of Rome. Under the terms of this Directive all member states had to have passed relevant national legislation by 1992 incorporating its terms. In the case of the UK this occurred via the Financial Services Act 1991.

An important complementary measure arising from Directive 85/611 is the provision of a uniform measure of protection for investors under the UCITS umbrella.

In practice barriers still exist which prevent the free marketing of financial and investment services in member states, a matter which the proposed Directive on Investment Services hopes to address. Under this Directive it is proposed that once the home member state has granted the necessary approval, the organization concerned will be allowed to establish its business in the other eleven states irrespective of any national regulations regarding what firms can sell and how their products may be marketed.

8

Other internal policies

Introduction

The subjects of the previous two chapters on the single market and economic and monetary policy relate strongly to the original nature of the European *Economic* Community. However, as became clear in chapter 3 on the European Treaties, since the Treaty of Rome was signed the Community has become active in a very much wider range of areas of life. This fundamental change in the nature of the Community was symbolized with the official change in its name from European Economic Community (EEC) to European Community (EC) in the Maastricht Treaty of 1991.

   This chapter sets out briefly the major provisions of European policy in five important areas. It is not a comprehensive description of the entire range of the Community's activities, but will give you an idea of the scope of Community interests and powers in the affairs of its member states.

The Common Agricultural Policy

The Common Agricultural Policy (CAP) prevents prices of the main agricultural commodities, eg cereals, milk and lamb, being determined by the interaction of market forces, ie supply and demand.

Objectives

- to provide a minimum income for the European farming community
- to provide uniform agricultural prices throughout the EC
- to prevent one member state gaining competitive advantage over another due to the effect of agricultural prices on wage rates and unit costs of production
- to stabilize fluctuations in agricultural supplies and prices to consumers resulting from the vagaries of the annual harvests
- to raise agricultural productivity and release resources for other sectors of the economy

Mechanisms

- maintenance of income for farmers via common external tariff, preventing inflow of cheap agricultural products from non-EC states
- maintenance of income for farmers via official support (buying and selling) mechanisms in order to maintain the current agricultural support price levels (intervention)

The CAP in Practice

Agriculture was one of the first industries to recover after the Second World War. Technology, both in terms of equipment and in terms of ways of improving the land, resulted in significant increases in production. However, increases in income for farmers did not follow automatically; agriculture, in large part because of its dependence on external factors such as weather, remains a notoriously volatile industry.

Despite being one of the most nearly completed common policies of the Community, the CAP has caused perhaps the greatest difficulties for member states of any policy area. Expenditure on CAP has taken a disproportionately large share of Community expenditure; but efforts to reform the policy in such a way as to reduce this share have been fiercely resisted by those who benefit from its support. Conflict between member states with highly mechanized agricultural sectors and those with more traditional farming methods has been a feature of the many attempts at CAP reform.

Many of the problems which beset the CAP in the early years of the Community stemmed from fluctuations in exchange rates, which should stabilize with the introduction of the ERM. A turning point was the decision in March 1984 that expenditure via the CAP should be limited. Not to do so, it was agreed, would bankrupt the Community. Reforms have continued since that time, but never free from controversy. Over-production has been tackled by the extremely controversial 'set aside' scheme, whereby farmers are paid *not* to produce from all their land.

This policy seems to please no one: farmers, agribusinesses and environmentalists are united in their distaste for it.

The CAP will no doubt continue to be high on the agenda of the Community for many years to come.

Home Affairs, Justice and Immigration

Matters within these areas were deliberated on at Maastricht and are set out in a supplementary protocol, not in the Treaty on European Union itself. The protocol sets out areas of common interest:

- Asylum policy
- Controls on external borders
- Immigration policy for nationals of non-EC states
- Combating drug addiction
- Combating fraud
- Judicial cooperation in civil matters
- Judicial cooperation in criminal matters
- Customs cooperation
- Police cooperation and the creation of Europol

The Treaty goes on to say that the areas of common interest identified shall be dealt with in compliance with the European Convention on Human Rights and Fundamental Freedoms.

Member states agree to consult one another with a view to coordinating action in these areas.

Employment, Social Affairs and Education

The Social Chapter

The Social Chapter of the Maastricht Treaty epitomizes the widening and deepening of the Community's areas of concern to cover matters previously considered the preserve of individual counties. Indeed, at the Maastricht summit in December 1991 the British government refused to accept the Social Chapter of the Treaty on the grounds that the matters contained within it were matters of national not Community competence. The other 11 member states therefore signed a protocol to adopt these articles which were not included in the Treaty itself. Those 11 member states confirmed their wish to implement the 1989 Social Charter (see chapter 2) and agreed the following protocol on social policy.

Article 1

The Community and member states shall have as their objectives the promotion of employment, improved living and working conditions, proper social protection, dialogue between management and labour, the development of human resources with a view to lasting high employment and the combating of exclusion. To this end the Community and member states shall implement measures which take account of the diverse forms of national practices, in particular in the field of contractual relations and the need to maintain the competitiveness of the Community economy.

Article 2

Commits the Community to support member states in the following fields:

- working conditions
- the informing and consultation of workers
- equality of treatment between men and women
- the integration of persons excluded from the labour market

Progress in these areas is to be achieved by the implementation of Directives.

Additionally, operating unanimously, the Council of Ministers shall act in the following areas:

- social security and social protection of workers
- protection of workers when their employment contract is terminated
- representation and collective defence of the interests of workers and employers
- conditions of employment for non-Community nationals legally resident in a member state
- financial contribution for promotion of employment and job creation

The provisions of Article 2 do not apply to pay, the right of association, the right to strike or the right to impose lock-outs.

Article 3

Deals with the promotion of consultation between management and labour at Community level.

Article 4

Deals with the eventual promotion of contractual relations and agreements between management and labour.

Article 5

Encourages cooperation among member states and coordination of their action in all social policy fields.

Article 6

States that each member country shall ensure that the principle of equal pay for male and female workers for equal work is applied.

It also provides for appropriate positive measures to be taken to make it easier for women to pursue a vocational activity or to prevent or compensate for disadvantages in their professional careers.

Article 7

Provides for the Commission to draw up an annual report on progress to achieving the objectives set out in Article 1.

The European citizen

The Maastricht Treaty set out for the first time the rights in respect of the Community possessed by every individual who is a national of a member state. Article 8 of the Treaty:

- creates citizenship of the European Union, and gives it to every person holding the nationality of a member state
- gives free movement for citizens within the Community, subject to the existing conditions in the Treaty of Rome
- gives each citizen the right to stand and vote in municipal elections in the member state in which he or she resides (not to come into effect until details are adopted by member states before 31 December 1994)
- gives the citizen the right to stand and vote in elections for the European Parliament in the member state in which he or she resides
- gives the citizen the protection of diplomatic authorities of any member state when he or she is in a third country where his or her own country does not have representation
- gives the right to petition the European Parliament and use the European Ombudsman.

Education, vocational training and youth matters

Articles 126 and 127 of the Maastricht Treaty set out the following principles.

The Community shall contribute to the development of quality education by encouraging cooperation between member states whilst respecting their rights to organize their own education systems.

In particular, the Community shall aim to:

- develop the European dimension in education
- encourage mobility of teachers and students, especially by the mutual recognition of diplomas and periods of study
- develop exchanges of information and experience
- encourage exchanges of young people and socio-educational instructors
- encourage the development of distance learning.

The Community shall implement a vocational training policy.

Community action shall aim to:

- facilitate industrial changes through vocational training and retraining
- improve vocational training in order to facilitate vocational integration and reintegration into the labour market
- facilitate access to vocational training and encourage mobility
- stimulate cooperation on training between educational or training establishments and firms
- develop exchanges of information and experience.

The Community and member states shall foster cooperation with third countries and competent international organizations in the sphere of vocational training.

Culture

Article 128 of the Maastricht Treaty states that:

The Community shall contribute to the flowering of the cultures of the member states while respecting their national and regional diversity and at the same time bringing the common cultural heritage to the fore.

Action by the Community shall be aimed at encouraging cooperation between member states and if necessary supporting and supplementing their actions in the following areas:

- improvement of the knowledge and dissemination of the culture and history of the European peoples
- conservation and safeguarding of cultural heritage of European significance
- non-commercial cultural exchanges
- artistic and literary creation including the audio-visual sector

The Environment, Health and Consumer Protection

Protecting the Environment

Article 130 of the Maastricht Treaty identifies the following central objectives in the community policy on the environment:

- preserving, protecting and improving the quality of the environment
- protecting human health
- prudent and rational utilization of natural resources
- promoting international measures to deal with environmental problems

The policy is based on the principle that preventative action should be taken, that environmental damage should be rectified at source and that the polluter should pay.

Member states are not prevented from introducing measures more stringent than those of the Community, so long as these are notified to the Commission and are not incompatible with the Treaty.

Public Health

Article 129 of the Maastricht Treaty states that the Community 'shall contribute towards ensuring a high level of human health protection by encouraging cooperation between member states and, if necessary, lending support to their action. Community action shall be directed towards the prevention of diseases, in particular the major health scourges including drug dependence, by promoting research into their causes and their transmission as well as health information and education.'

Article 129 also provides for the harmonization of laws, the introduction of regulations and the adoption of incentives to contribute to the achievement of these aims. The provisions of the Treaty therefore envisage greater cooperation among member states to prevent drug addiction and the spread of Aids.

The Council of Ministers will be able to adopt recommendations in the public health field by qualified majority voting, and member states will under the Treaty coordinate their public health programmes and policies with the European Commission.

Consumer Protection

Article 127A of the Maastricht Treaty states that:

- The Community shall contribute to a high level of consumer protection through measures adopted through Article 100A. Article 100A relates to the adoption by qualified majority voting of measures to harmonize national law in order to complete the internal market

- The Community shall take specific action in addition to that undertaken in member states to protect the health, safety and economic interests of consumers and to provide them with adequate information
- Member states may introduce more stringent measures as long as they are not incompatible with the Treaty and the Commission is informed

Transport and Communications

The original Treaty of Rome contained numerous provisions about the creation of a common European transport policy. Harmonization of transport was seen as a cornerstone of the creation of an energetic and prosperous internal market.

However, transport policy failed to be implemented holistically by member states in the early years of the Community, and was allowed to develop only patchily; protectionist practice remained (and still remains) in this area of community activity.

The main provisions of Community policy on transport are contained in Articles 74–84 of the Treaty of Rome. The terms in which the Treaty sets out the transport policy are noticeably more vague than the terms in which other policies are set out.

Article 75
    The Council shall . . . by a qualified majority lay down . . .
    (a)   common rules applicable to international transport to or from the territory of a member state . . .
    (b)   the conditions under which non-resident carriers may operate transport services within a member state.

Article 76
    Prohibits discrimination by member states against carriers of other member states

Article 77
    Enables states, however, to subsidize transport as a public service or for the purposes of coordination

---

Deregulation of transport and the creation of an internal market in transport services was seen by the Commission as one of the key factors in the establishment of free movement of goods across the Community.

From 1 January 1993 road hauliers (previously one of the groups which suffered most from the costs of non-Europe) have complete freedom to carry out international journeys within the Community.

Problems still remain however in relation to cabotage, a system which allows a haulier to pick up goods in member state other than his own and transport them within that member state. Delays in the implementation of a completely free internal market in road transport after 1 January 1993 have been caused by France and Germany holding up the deregulation of road haulage by insisting on the harmonization of road taxes. In the meantime the right of a road haulier in one member state operating in another member state may still be restricted by the requirement of a licence to transport goods being obtained from that member state.

Figure 8.1 French lorry drivers eat lunch while their trucks block the Paris-Lille A1 road – July 1992
Source: *Associated Press/Topham*

Trans-European Networks

The Maastricht Treaty introduced the concept of trans-European networks in the areas of transport, telecommunications and energy infrastructure in order to enable citizens of the European Union, economic operators and regional and local communities to derive the full benefit from the setting up of an area without internal frontiers.

It stated that the Community should contribute towards the establishment of these networks, aiming to promote the interconnection and interoperability of national networks as well as access to common European networks. It also noted that particular account needed to be taken of the need to link island, landlocked and peripheral regions with the central regions of the Community.

Energy

The coordination and development of safe energy policies was an important element of the philosophy behind the establishment of the EEC in the 1950s. The Schuman Plan adopted by the original six signatories to the Treaty of Rome was designed to create a common market for coal and steel and was signed by the six in Paris on 18 April 1951. It prohibited import and export duties on these products and measures having equivalent effect, as well as outlawing discriminatory and restrictive practices in the coal and steel industries.

At the same time as the Treaty of Rome establishing the European Economic Community was signed on 25 March 1957, a second treaty was signed which provided for the establishment of the European Atomic Energy Community, or EURATOM. This institution was set up in oder to ensure the peaceful development of nuclear energy on a pan-European basis. The UK (not a signatory) had a well developed atomic energy capability and the six signatories to EURATOM saw their cooperation as a way of ensuring that they kept up with the UK from both the technological and the safety point of view.

The Brussels Treaty of 1965 (otherwise known as the Merger Treaty) had the effect of combining the Economic, Coal and Steel, and Atomic Energy Communities into the same institutional framework.

In recent years the common energy policies of the Community have faded from the spotlight as more emphasis has come to be placed on the development of economic policies and the establishment of the Single Market. However, the Maastricht Treaty provides for the establishment of Trans-European Networks (see above) and envisages that technological and other barriers shall be dismantled in order to ensure the development of networks in the areas of transport, telecommunications and energy.

The Treaty envisages that the Cohesion Fund (which exists to boost the economies of poorer or remoter areas of the Community) could be used to finance the establishment of such networks by the provision of loans, guarantees and feasibility studies.

For the EC Cohesion Fund see chapter 7

The Maastricht Treaty provides for new policies to be laid down in the field of energy, but made no detailed provisions. A report will be forthcoming from the Commission in 1996. It is anticipated that this report will lay an increasing emphasis on renewable energy sources, environmentally sound energy policies and conservation of energy.

9

The EC and the wider world

Introduction: Fortress Europe?

There is a view of the EC according to which the Community is a club of rich, developed countries, an elite whose members jealously guard their own interests and whose energies are devoted to helping each other, turning their collective back on the rest of the world. This has been called the 'Fortress Europe' syndrome. Nothing could be further from the truth.

This chapter examines the EC's relationships with the world outside its boundaries from two perspectives:

- first, that of foreign and security policy – how the EC can forge a shared approach to matters affecting the stance in the world and the security of its member states;

- second, that of trade and aid relations – how the EC relates to other actors and organizations in the world economy: GATT, the USA and Japan, EFTA; and to other groups of countries, specifically the countries of eastern Europe and those of the developing world.

The Common Foreign and Security Policy

Chapter J of the Maastricht Treaty states: 'A common foreign and security policy is hereby established.' The objectives of such a policy are identified as follows:

- to safeguard the common values, fundamental interests and independence of the union
- to strengthen the security of the union and its member states in all ways
- to preserve peace and strengthen international security
- to promote international cooperation
- to develop and consolidate democracy and the role of law, and respect for human rights and fundamental freedoms.

The EC's common foreign and security policy is intended to operate in a different way from other Community policies, as a result of compromises which were made at the Maastricht summit. In a federal state such as the USA or Germany, foreign and security policies are a matter for the federal authorities, not for the individual state (in the USA) or *Land* (in Germany). This is not the situation with the European Community, even though the Maastricht Treaty states that when it is ratified, a common foreign and security policy is thereby created.

If the common foreign and security policy had been made a policy of the Community in the same way as, for example, competition policy, that would mean that member states would be subjecting themselves in this important area to the supervision of the institution of the Community, notably the European Court of Justice. This would be a radical step for the member states to take. The ability of a national state to determine its own foreign and security policy is an important measure of its sovereign status. For example, countries 'recognize' new states – on independence, or after revolutions or divisions, as in the recognition of the countries which have emerged from the former Yugoslavia. In this recognition lies the assumption that as a sovereign state a country can 'confer' sovereign status on another country. Any question, therefore, of surrendering (or even pooling) sovereignty in this area to an EC institution was likely to be resisted very strongly. Therefore, although the Maastricht Treaty contains provisions which establish a common foreign and security policy, it is important to understand that in practice what was agreed at Maastricht was a compromise between national traditions and sensitivities, on the one hand, and the 'European ideal' on the other.

According to the agreement that was reached at Maastricht, the European Council may agree joint EC action in a particular foreign policy area. The Treaty does not imply that *all* foreign policy should be so decided. Once a particular policy stance has been agreed then the policy will be implemented jointly and without an individual member state being able to veto the implementation. What matters come within the scope of the joint action is for the Council to decide.

In a case of what the Treaty calls an 'imperative need' where the situation has changed and the Council has not acted, member states may take necessary measures as a matter of urgency and inform the Council immediately.

The Common Defence Policy

The formulation of a common EC defence policy is complicated not only by the membership of certain of the member states in NATO, but also by the existence of the defence-oriented organization the Western European Union, which includes nine of the 12 EC member states (excluding Denmark, Greece and Ireland).

In view of these existing obligations, the Maastricht Treaty arrived at the following statements:

- the common foreign and security policy shall include all questions related to the security of the union, including the eventual framing of a common defence policy which might in time lead to a common defence (Article J4)
- the policy of the WEU shall respect NATO obligations and not prejudice national policies in this area
- there shall be an IGC in 1996 to discuss this area of policy further
- the WEU shall have a strengthened role on the defence component of the union
- member states not in the WEU shall be invited to join

The EC and GATT

GATT (the General Agreement on Tariffs and Trade) was founded after the Second World War with the objective of opening up and freeing world trade in order to boost the world economy. By 1992 it had 111 members. GATT works on the principles of eliminating protective trade barriers and making multilateral agreements amongst member states which do not discriminate against any of its members. It also functions as a negotiating body should any trade disputes or problems occur between its members, and helps to establish the rules for the conduct of world trade.

The European Commission negotiates within GATT to represent the 12 member states. GATT holds rounds of talks which culminate every few years in an agreement on specific categories of goods. The rounds can take several years to complete. There have been seven rounds to date, the most famous of which are the Kennedy, Nixon, Tokyo and, most recently, the Uruguay round. The latter has been rather controversial. Started in 1986, it aimed amongst other things to extend GATT policies to agricultural products. This immediately sparked a conflict between the EC and the US representatives. The USA objected to the large subsidies enjoyed by European farmers, suggesting that these represented an unfair advantage in world trade over US farmers. Negotiations over the subsidies staggered on over several years, only to flounder spectacularly in November 1992.

Internal wrangling and disagreements amongst EC members affected adversely the Community's ability to negotiate effectively. The USA, tiring of the delay in reaching an agreement, seized the initiative and forced the EC to conclude the negotiations or face the threat of a trade war. A tentative agreement was reached at the end of 1992, but the episode inevitably soured US–EC relations, reviving the accusations of 'Fortress Europe'. Suggestions that the EC is prepared to deal with external trading nations only on its own terms must inevitably harm the global trading environment.

GATT is a worldwide organization which takes into account all of its members' wishes, even though on occasion some members, such as the USA and the EC, figure particularly prominently in negotiations. GATT will inevitably play a major role in the world trade pattern of the 1990s.

The EC, the USA and Japan

From the viewpoint of the USA, the European single market programme can be viewed both as an opportunity and as a threat. For many multinational companies (whether American or Japanese) that have already established a base in Europe, the EC internal market represents a major business opportunity for the 1990s and beyond. Other companies, particularly medium-sized enterprises, may see it as a threat. It may become tougher for such companies to export into the EC should the external frontiers become more difficult to penetrate. As the EC has enjoyed a trading surplus with the USA in recent years, it would appear that the Community holds many aces.

The EC's trading relationship with Japan shows the reverse pattern. Japan is gradually being persuaded to open up its markets more and more to European goods, but the Japanese still enjoy a significant trade surplus with the Community. The EC is a very important market for the Japanese, who have been anxious to preserve this. They have gained access to EC markets by building factories in the member states, thereby stimulating the local economies and gaining the advantage of operating from within the Community itself. The EC had instigated a series of measures against Japanese companies imposing anti-dumping duties on them, suggesting that the Japanese are attempting to avoid anti-dumping duties on the import of goods by building their factories in EC countries, using cheap Japanese components and therefore gaining an unfair advantage over member states' own industries. The east/west struggle for business supremacy continues with the Japanese in the lead.

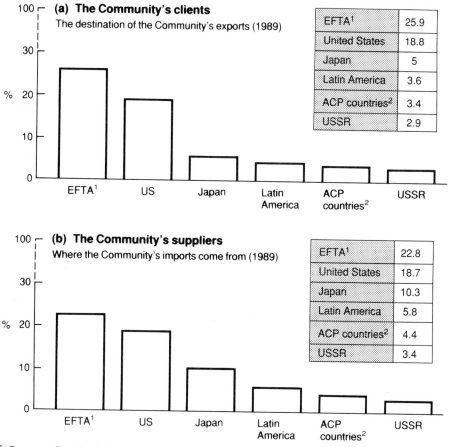

(a) The Community's clients The destination of the Community's exports (1989)	
EFTA[1]	25.9
United States	18.8
Japan	5
Latin America	3.6
ACP countries[2]	3.4
USSR	2.9

(b) The Community's suppliers Where the Community's imports come from (1989)	
EFTA[1]	22.8
United States	18.7
Japan	10.3
Latin America	5.8
ACP countries[2]	4.4
USSR	3.4

[1] European Free Trade Association (Austria, Switzerland, Iceland, Sweden, Norway, Finland).

[2] Countries in Africa, the Caribbean and the Pacific, which have ties with the Community through the Lomé Convention.

Figure 9.1 The Community's trading partners

In the late 1980s the EC promoted the policy of 'Reciprocity' with its trading partners. On the surface it is a simple and fair concept: in everyday terms it means 'let me have access to your market and you can have access to mine'. Undoubtedly this principle would work in many circumstances; but it has run into trouble with the USA. Adoption of reciprocity would mean that EC businesses could operate in any of the US states and the USA could, if it wanted to, operate anywhere in Europe – a simple swap of privileges. However, some industries in the USA, e.g. banking, are quite severely constrained by state law; they are not free to operate anywhere in the USA, but are restricted to their own state. Consequently, under the reciprocity terms, European banks would be able to open branches anywhere in the USA, whereas an American bank could not. The Europeans would then have a distinct advantage over US banks in their home market – an unsatisfactory arrangement for the Americans. The problems are many and are still being examined. The EC has stated that Europe wishes to be a partner in world trade rather than a hostile guardian of its own boundaries. Only time will tell if this is true.

Figure 9.2 Japanese factory based in Hounslow
Source: *Robert Harding Picture Library*

The EC, EFTA and the EEA

The European Free Trade Association was founded in 1960 by Austria, Denmark, Norway, Portugal, Sweden, Switzerland and the UK as a response to the then fledgling EEC. It was, as its name indicates, primarily a free trade association and initially the UK hoped that the EEC would seek membership of EFTA. This would enable the UK and Europe to trade freely without harming the trade of the Commonwealth countries whose interests the UK was hoping to preserve. This proposal was unlikely to succeed, and by 1961 the UK had decided that its future lay with that of the

EEC and had made its first application for membership. EFTA continued, however, and today the EC and EFTA are very important trading partners. EFTA comprises seven industrialized and wealthy countries: Austria, Finland, Iceland, Liechtenstein, Norway, Sweden and Switzerland. All of these countries could undoubtedly contribute to the EC if they were member states, and all have already applied for EC membership.

The close relationship between the EC and EFTA culminated in the creation in 1991 of the EEA (European Economic Area). This agreement created a trading bloc of 19 countries (12 EC states plus the seven EFTA members) and allowed the EFTA countries to join the single market programme on 1 January 1993, enjoying the benefits of free movement of goods, services, capital and labour. EFTA will also follow EC legislation on company and consumer law as well as education and social policy.

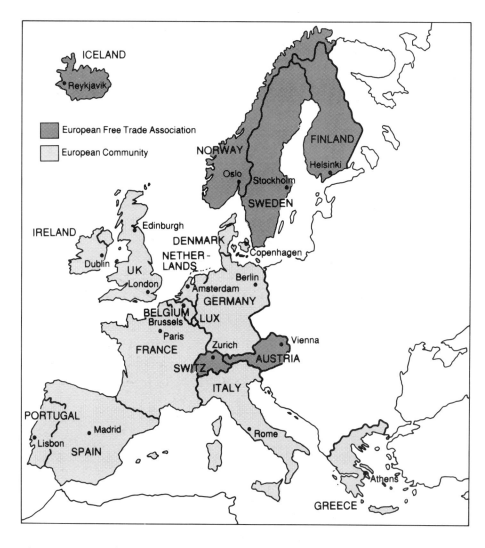

Figure 9.3 EC and EFTA countries at a glance

The potential of this trading bloc should not be underestimated: it will account for nearly 50% of global trade. Cynics point out that the EFTA states have had an easy ride: they will benefit from access to the EC markets, but have avoided contributing to the problem areas in the EC such as the Common Agricultural Policy. However, they have had to pay for the privilege of access to the single market. EFTA is lending 1.5 billion Ecu and donating 500 million Ecu to a fund to help the poorer EC countries. It has also granted extra fishing rights in Norwegian waters to Spain and Portugal up until 1997. In return, EFTA countries have been provided with safeguards, particularly around foreign ownership of banks, financial institutions and real estate, for a limited period.

Both parties will benefit from the arrangement. It remains to be seen whether the division of spoils will be unfair. The first signs of problems ahead emerged in December 1992, just before the start of the single market, when the Swiss people voted 'no' in a referendum on membership of the EEA. This has led to a temporary halt in the process and it is likely that the EFTA countries will not now be in a position to participate in the single market until the Swiss problem is sorted out.

If any disputes arise in the future within a fully operating EEA, a court linked to the European Court of Justice had already been set up to settle them.

The EC and Eastern Europe

Post-1989 Europe is a turbulent and dynamic continent with the struggle for democracy in the countries of the former communist bloc causing shock waves and ripples throughout the Community. After the euphoria of gaining freedom from external or internal oppressors, the construction of alternative systems has been far from easy. Formerly suppressed conflicts have come to the surface, most appallingly in the war in what used to be Yugoslavia. The EC has helped out with aid, but for the present can do little more.

The stage is now set, however, for the question of a much wider Europe. Many East European countries and former Soviet republics have applied for membership of the EC, including Estonia, Latvia, Lithuania, Poland, Hungary, and Bulgaria and (before partition) Czechoslovakia as well as Malta and Cyprus (and the EFTA countries – see above). It is difficult to predict when and how many of these countries will ever realize EC membership, particularly when the existing EC is beset by so many internal problems in agreeing the way forward after Maastricht. However, European agreements have already been reached with Hungary, Czechoslovakia and Poland, the countries in which the reform process is most advanced. These agreements work towards abolition of quotas and give preferential treatment in trade. It is hoped that this process will gradually extend to other countries as the political system allows it.

The EC and Developing Countries

It has always been one of the EC's objectives to promote links with the worldwide community. Article 110 of the Treaty of Rome contains the commitment in principle to

C ontribute, in the common interest, to the harmonious development of world trade, the progressive abolition of restrictions in international trade and the lowering of customs barriers.

TRADE, AID AND COOPERATION AGREEMENTS

1958   European Development Fund created
Purpose: to work for the fulfilment of Article 110 of the Treaty of Rome

1963   Yaounde Convention signed, including 18 African countries and Madagascar
Purpose: to provide aid to the African region

1975   First Lomé Convention signed, including 69 African, Caribbean and Pacific countries
Purpose: to give help in emergencies and to foster long-term development

1979   Second Lomé Convention

1984   Third Lomé Convention

1989   Fourth Lomé Convention

The European Development Fund created in 1958 was set up for this purpose, followed in 1963 by the Yaounde Convention (see box).

The Lomé Conventions

The first Lomé Convention was signed in 1975 by the EC and 46 African, Caribbean and Pacific (ACP) countries; the fourth, in 1989, was signed by the then 12 member states and 69 ACP countries. Many of these countries have close links with member states, particularly those which are ex-colonies.

The Lomé Convention is the largest single aid programme in the world and is negotiated and updated at regular intervals. It aims to give help in emergencies but simultaneously to work towards long-term development. Its objectives, to be achieved through a process of negotiation, are:

- to promote rural development and combat hunger
- to strengthen partners' economies and lessen dependence
- to gain lasting improvements to people's living standards.

Lomé IV is intended to cover the ten-year period from 1990 to 2000. It has three main elements: Trade, aid and cooperation. The EC is to give 12 billion Ecu worth of aid in the form of loans and grants over the first five years. This aid is non-repayable, apart from risk capital and loans from the European Investment Bank. Lomé also grants preferential access to EC markets for ACP products: such access to the world's richest markets should provide a boost to each ACP country's economy. There are also benefits for the EC under this system: EC exports into ACP countries enjoy 'most favoured nation' (MFN) status, which gives them preferential access to ACP markets.

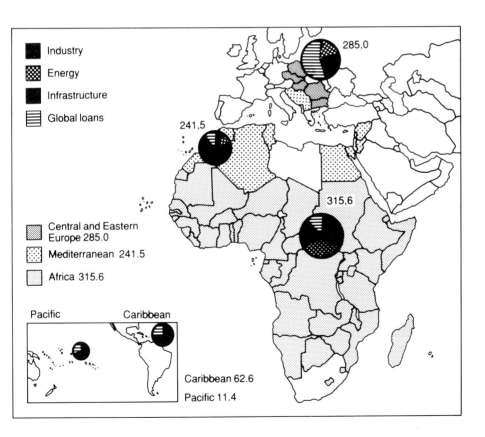

Figure 9.4 Financing provided outside the Community in 1991 (million Ecus)
Source: *European Investment Bank*

The Lomé programme is one which allows the developing countries considerable self-direction. It is a politically neutral programme which promotes cooperation between governments of differing political opinions. It works on the principle of allowing the ACP countries a great degree of self-determination in the allocation of aid. Power is shared between the EC and ACP countries, with joint decision-making on particular projects. The whole system is underwritten by a continuous dialogue between the EC and ACP governments and institutions allowing for cooperation and progress.

Latin America

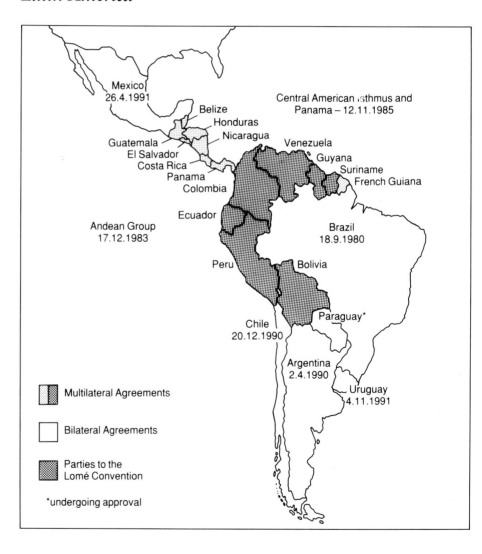

Figure 9.5 Cooperation agreements with the countries of Latin America (each partner's name is followed by the date on which the relevant agreement was signed)

Links between the EC and Latin America have multiplied and strengthened dramatically over the last two decades. The first wave of cooperation agreements between the EC and Latin America were made in the 1970s with Brazil and Uruguay and concerned trade alone. The third-generation agreements of the 1990s encompass the whole mainland, and cover a much wider range of topics, some of which are particularly pertinent to that continent – as well as trade, the environment and the containment of the drugs problem. There is also provision for economic, industrial, scientific and technical cooperation; and the region has also been the recipient of food and humanitarian aid.

Latin America is a key future market for the EC, accounting for 20% of both the EC's imports and exports. This has resulted in Latin America using the *Generalized System of Preferences* for its trade which grants it easier access to European markets for its products.

This system also aims to encourage and support the exporting policies of the exporting countries, and its use should foster the development of the existing promising situation into an excellent and thriving long-term trading relationship.

Asia

Agreements broadly similar to those made with Latin American countries have been made between the EC and several Asian countries. Asian countries are entitled to preferential treatment under the EC's Generalized System of Preferences for exports from developing countries and to financial aid from the EC budget.

A regional agreement was made in 1980 with ASEAN (The Association of South East Asian Nations), whose members today comprise Brunei, Indonesia, Malaysia, the Philippines, Singapore and Thailand. This established a framework for business, economic and development cooperation. The framework allows for continuous dialogue, with particular emphasis on the promotion of European investment in the region.

The Mediterranean

The countries bordering the Mediterranean Sea have a natural trading link with the EC because of their proximity and shared history. It is also vital to the EC that this area remains stable, both economically and politically, so it is very much in the interests of the EC to promote sound links which foster prosperity within this region. The 1960s saw the first limited agreements and by 1975 cooperation agreements had been concluded with Morocco, Algeria, Tunisia, Egypt, Jordan, Syria and the Lebanon.

The EC and the Mediterranean countries have much to gain from an interdependent relationship. The EC exports US$30 billion worth of goods and services into the Mediterranean and receives goods worth US$ 25 billion back, making the Mediterranean a more significant trading partner than Japan. Most Mediterranean countries depend heavily on exporting to the EC. There is also a large-scale movement into the EC from these countries of people seeking work.

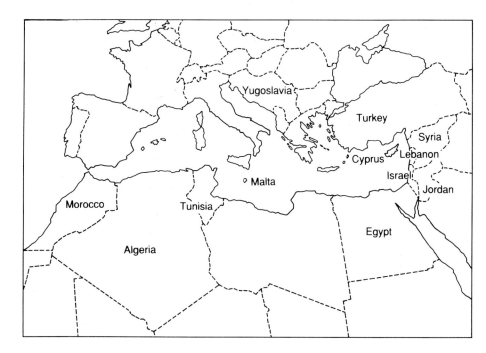

Figure 9.6 Mediterranean countries that have concluded agreements with the Community

FACTFILE ON THE EC'S AID PROGRAMME

- 107 Third World countries have cooperation agreements with the EC

- In 1988 EC development aid amounted to US$2.9 billion, which accounts for 5.4% of EC expenditure

- Aid from the EC and the individual member states accounts for 36% of world aid

- Major beneficiaries of Community aid:

Sub-Saharan Africa	63.0%
Southern Asia	12.3%
Latin America and the Caribbean	11.1%

  Development projects account for 64% of this aid and food aid for 23%

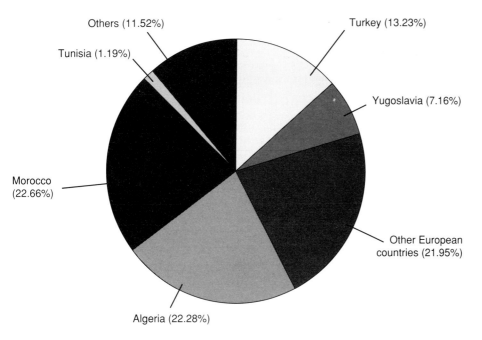

Figure 9.7 Employees within the EC from non-Community countries (1988)

The EC wishes to encourage the Mediterranean countries to become more self-reliant in terms of development, and towards this end the Community implemented the New Mediterranean Policy in 1990. This policy aims to support and encourage the Mediterranean countries in moves towards a freer economic system and a more democratic political system. The policy was being put to the test in 1993 in war-torn Yugoslavia where the EC has endeavoured to help in many ways. The policy was supported by an aid package of 4,405 million Ecu.

part four

THE EC INTO THE TWENTY-FIRST CENTURY

10

The EC – Where Next?

This chapter covers four main themes in the Community's future:
- The size of the Community and its internal relationships
- European culture in an enlarged Community
- The future of the EMS and progress towards economic and monetary union
- Environmental issues

The View towards the 21st Century

As the last decade of this century passes, what kind of future can we anticipate for Europe? Some areas of Community activity involve a lot of forward planning – moves towards monetary union, for example – and here it may be possible to make predictions with some degree of confidence. But elsewhere uncertainties abound, and forecasts seem little better than speculation. In early 1993:

- neither the UK nor Denmark had yet ratified the Maastricht Treaty
- Europe was in the grip of a deep recession, with many observers seeing no likely economic upturn until well into 1994
- refugees were flooding into the Community for both political and economic reasons
- the spectre of extreme nationalism was becoming more and more visible
- the former Yugoslavia was in bloody turmoil
- the countries of Eastern Europe were attempting to implement political and economic reform, with varying degrees of confidence and success.

In such circumstances, to suggest what the state of the Community might be in five or ten years' time might seem simply foolhardy. What this chapter does, then, rather than trying to make firm predictions, is to raise some of the questions that will be central to the direction taken by the EC, and to point out some of the issues that the Community will have to grapple with before the end of the 20th century in order to move with confidence into the 21st.

Even this approach, however, must be recognized for what it is: an attempt to look into as yet unwritten pages of history. Issues have a habit of disappearing, like hills, the closer you get to them; and hazards that no one has anticipated can prove to be serious stumbling blocks.

None the less, an institution such as the European Community is by its very nature dynamic and cannot stand still, any more than the wider world will cease to develop and change. It is therefore very important to look towards the future, not only in order to be in some measure prepared for whatever it brings, but in order to be able to take a hand in shaping that future.

A Greater Europe?

In the past the European Community has made its most rapid strides when it has had key issues to drive it forward. A focus has tended to galvanize all of its member states into action, harnessing their energies and effort. Recent major foci of attention for the Community have been the push towards completion of the single market programme in January 1993 and the Treaty on European Union (the Maastricht Treaty). Assuming that the Maastricht Treaty is ratified and implemented, the next major stimulus, which will impel the Community into the 21st Century, will probably be the debate over the enlargement of the Community, either by extending its membership to other states or by deepening the ways in which existing member states are commited to the European union.

Widening v. deepening

If the Community moves towards widening then new states will be encouraged to join, increasing membership from the current 12 up to a possible total of 25 members. Many states have already applied for membership, and interest in joining is strong both in Scandinavia and amongs the fledgling democracies of Eastern Europe. January 1993 marked the beginning of the official negotiations on proposed membership with Austria, Norway, Finland and Sweden. It is anticipated that the negotiations and necessary Treaties of Accession with these four countries will have been completed by January 1995.

This enlargement of the Community from 12 to 16 members by 1995 and possibly to 25 members by 2001 will force discussion on the role of existing EC institutions and heighten the debate on the concept of 'federalism'. It has been said that many existing member states prefer the option of deepening the EC to widening it; the President of the Commission, Jacques Delors, also prefers this direction as deepening implies progress towards federalism – concentrating on stronger union amongst current member states, moving towards a more integrated Europe, rather than welcoming a large number of new members.

Deepening obviously has serious political implications which centre on national sovereignty. This has aroused anxieties, even hostility, in some member states: notably the UK, which favours a larger, looser Community. Margaret Thatcher, indeed, was said to have used the widening issue as a smokescreen which would prevent Europe moving towards any type of federal union.

Potential recruits obviously favour the widening option, although some, particularly Hungary, do not see the principles of widening and deepening as being mutually exclusive. Hungary takes the view that there need not be any contradiction between the two goals. Whether this is a viable position remains to be seen.

The widening versus deepening issue is contentious for economic, political and social reasons – both amongst existing members and among those who hope to join. The debate could well provoke the greatest controversy since the creation of the EEC in 1957, and the current situation in European affairs does not suggest that rapid progress will be made towards agreement in this area. A 1992 opinion poll in Austria showed a majority in favour of a looser economic structure with strong views against any movement that would create a close political union in areas such as foreign policy. The recent Swiss refusal, following a referendum, to join the European Economic Area has effectively terminated the hope of total free trade area across the whole continent.

For the EEA see chapter 7

Widening versus deepening is an issue with which the Community has to come to grips. The collapse of communism in East Europe has lent urgency to the debate and accelerated the movement towards enlargement. Neither the Community nor the larger Western Europe can afford to ignore Eastern Europe, politically or economically. The overall objective for the whole continent (which includes some of the former Soviet republics) must be to evolve into a stable and secure region, enjoying economic prosperity and political harmony. The EC needs therefore to build a Community with this as its objective.

Two-speed Europe?

The Maastricht-Treaty was envisaged by its original proponents as just one stop on the road towards total European union – a federal Europe. Supporters of this view believed that the Treaty would help to prevent the Community developing on two separate routes, with the so-called 'fast-track' members, i.e. those most inclined towards union – especially Germany and France – dominating its future.

How are the aims of Maastricht to be reconciled with the choice between widening or deepening? To welcome new members may result in not just a two-speed but a three- or four-speed Europe. If the alternative is simply to concentrate on closer union amongst the 12, will the Community actually progress or will it continue to argue internally over greater integration, risking stagnation while it does so? A two-speed Europe may be better than a single slow-speed Europe. Some think that a series of bilateral accords with single citizenship and a single currency for those who wish it might be preferable to any feasible alternative.

However, EC finance ministers meeting in the autumn of 1992 came out against the idea of moving to monetary union at two speeds. The whole objective, they said, of monetary union was to proceed *together* towards fulfilling the convergence the criteria.

On the convergence criteria for monetary union, see chapter 7

Who might join, and why?

If the Community were to decide to adopt a policy of enlargement, who might the potential new members be and which of them would have priority for membership?

Countries currently considering potential membership fall into four main groups:

- The rich EFTA countries, e.g. Norway, Sweden, Austria and Finland. These countries' applications are already well advanced (see above).
- Those Eastern European states who already hold associate membership, e.g. Hungary, Poland, Bulgaria, the Czech Republic and Slovakia.
- Mediterranean states, e.g. Cyprus and Turkey.
- Some former Soviet republics. This last group see membership as a long-term goal, because their economies will need major revision and development in order to reach a standard commensurate with membership and eventual economic union.

In economic terms, it is acknowledged that the applicants most likely to be successful will be net contributors to the EC budget – probably the richer EFTA countries, as their economies are the most likely to meet EMU convergence criteria. Furthermore, these countries would not need to make demands on the cohesion funds. With such well-developed economies joining the prospect of increased trade and prosperity resulting from this enlarged single market will be very difficult to resist.

There are divisions within the Community as to how best to provide for enlargement as well as which countries to welcome. Current advocates of enlargement are Germany, the UK, France and Denmark. Spain is opposed, possibly fearing that poor East European entrants would attract EC development funds from which it might otherwise have expected to benefit. However, if the countries most likely to be given priority for membership are the rich EFTA countries, which would bring developed and prosperous economies into the Community and which would be likely to be net contributors to Community resources, then these fears are probably misplaced.

The EC does not appear yet to have established exactly what it will expect of its new members. Certainly those wishing to join the Community have different expectations of its benefits. Inevitably some states are keen to join what they see as a trade association; others are seeking the shelter of a common foreign and security policy. There are certain countries which do not seek full EC membership, but which would welcome access to the Community through cooperation in specific policies, such as transport and the environment. This 'à la carte' approach, where states could choose the policy areas in which they wished to cooperate on with the Community, has been called pragmatic by some and unrealistic by others. Until the Community decides in principle in which way it wishes to pursue the issue of enlargement, potential applicants can only speculate on the benefits they might receive on joining.

Enlargement: the implications

The timetable

The enlargement issue remained undecided in early 1993, mainly because of two major problem areas. The first is that the Maastricht Treaty on European Union had still not yet been ratified by all member states and therefore there were many constitutional problems within the existing EC to be resolved. The second is that the Delors 2 package (see chapter 7) encompassing income, expenditure and 'cohesion' funding increases is still being debated. Negotiations are expected to be completed by the end of 1993, but that still pushes the enlargement issue on to a back burner as the Community moves into the mid-1990s.

Structural changes

Whoever the new member states may be, it is likely that there would have to be both structural and institutional change within the EC to cope with the increased membership. A greater degree of centralism would be needed, with institutions such as a central bank to control and direct the enlarged Community. Questions of the power of European institutions such as the Commission and the Parliament would need to be redebated. Without some degree of increased control, it is unlikely that the enlarged Community could function or possibly even survive.

Some potential problems

Anticipating an enlarged Community, once membership has been decided, the EC still needs to overcome some problem areas.

1.   In social terms there are many issues to be considered. Much was made at the time the community was established of the fact that member states shared a common European culture. Could a greater Europe have the same cultural heritage? If not, would the mix of cultures be divisive or create unsurmountable difficulties – or does cultural diversity not matter?

2.   The current massive population shifts in Europe, involving both political refugees and so-called 'economic migrants' seeking work and prosperity, are being used and manipulated by the extreme right to fuel social unrest and disruption. The 'Fortress Europe' syndrome has reared its head again; but this time the goal is not to protect European trade and industry, but to prevent any further influx of immigrants into the Community. If the objective is to create an affluent Community, what will be the relationship between the EC and those countries who do not gain membership?

3.   If the poorer states of Eastern Europe do gain membership, might this encourage a rush of East European nationals using the free movement provisions to enter the more prosperous member states in search of prosperity? Would this then impede the economic and social development of those countries? Or will membership encourage East Europeans to stay at home and work on developing their own prosperity and that of their native land? This is an issue which will be of great concern to those states of Eastern Europe who are considering application for membership as well as to those Western states that border them.

The outlook for enlargement

The only likely brake to this process of enlargement could come from the current recession: the OECD predicted at the end of 1992 that there could be 34 million unemployed in Europe by the end of 1993. Economic hardship will undoubtedly slow down progress towards enlargement as member states concentrate their energies on the internal problems of generating recovery.

However, some objective and outside commentators on this debate have suggested that the current Community introspection over major policy directions, including enlargement, is sapping its energy and preventing it from growing into the world power that it could have become when the collapse of communism left a vacuum on the continent. Recent failures of the Community to act collectively and decisively in world affairs such as Somalia, the Gulf and Bosnia would seem to support this view.

European Culture

What is 'culture'?

The promotion of a common European culture is a theme much trumpeted by European unionists, who hail it as a bond unifying the member states of the Community. This is a difficult contention either to support or to disprove because of the very nature of the word 'culture'. What does it mean? It has to be more than an advanced state of intellectual and aesthetic achievement and must refer to broader points of common interests and values. Paradoxically, it could be argued, the degree of commonality increases the more narrowly one defines culture. Could 12 or 19 or 25 nations profess to share a common culture defined in either of these ways?

Generally, culture is taken to encompass the values and lifestyles that countries enjoy. It includes many elements, among them tradition; religion and history; heritage; social and sexual mores; ethnicity; attitudes towards children, families and work; acceptance of other races; education; and so on. Not all of these aspects may be common across even a whole member state: attitudes within individual countries can differ radically from one region to another, as seen for example in the different responses towards mixed-race marriages in northern and southern France.

Europe does not have a common culture in the sense of identical attitudes held in all member states. However, the member states do share many common bonds and some aspects of culture do cross national borders, weaving into the life of several countries and binding them together.

How much do Europeans share?

The question of a common European culture has been used by both sides in the federalism argument, with each side emphasizing similarities or differences in order to back up its position.

The federalists point to the 'ties that bind': common factors in the lives of Europeans. The sceptics not only emphasize the differences and make a virtue of diversity, but maintain that this diversity is threatened by the blandness of harmonization. These arguments are popularized in the UK by a tabloid press anxious to preserve the British pint and the British sausage from the clutches of Eurocrats who would make us drink beer or milk in 50 centilitre glasses and who would ban the Great British Banger. The 'Euro-sceptics' argue that a British national identity and a European culture are mutually exclusive and that we must choose between them. The idea that British national identity is *part of* European culture seems beyond their grasp.

The example of the USA, where clearly an American culture exists, but where individual states have quite distinct identities and lifestyles (witness the diversity of life between east and west Coast, Florida and New York State), would seem to disprove the sceptics' arguments. Those who hold this view, however, are not easily swayed by rational argument against what is essentially an emotional response.

Those who, on the other hand, claim that a common European culture exists which unites the Community will find it more difficult to support that claim should the enlargement of the EC become a reality. What cultural factors do the Scandinavian, Mediterranean and East Europe countries have in common with western Europe? Is a history of democracy is a prerequisite to a European culture? It seems unlikely. Culture surely consists of more than political structures. Perhaps we should argue that while these cultures are different, they will be complementary rather than conflicting. The richness and diversity of culture in each of the existing and proposed member states still permits of a unity of common cultural threads which cross national boundaries.

Respect for cultural differences

Differences between countries do exist and cannot be brushed aside. They can be seen particularly sharply when religion impacts on a country's culture and laws, as for example in Ireland's stance on abortion and contraception. The provision in EC law for states to withhold implementation of certain rules, for example the free movement of people, on the grounds of public policy, enables cultural differences to be accommodated. To use the same example, the Irish government does not permit freedom to establish abortion clinics in Ireland on the grounds of public policy, and this exclusion is permitted by the Community.

The mushrooming of satellite TV and pan-European broadcasting is already highlighting the major differences in sexual mores between EC countries. The broadcasting of pornography into countries whose laws forbid such transmissions is, at the beginning of 1993, a growing area of dispute. It is likely, however, that member states will be able to prohibit the broadcast of material considered unacceptable according to their national values.

A shared cultural past – and future

The ties that bind the European states have existed for over a thousand years. The ecclesiastical culture of the Middle Ages did not respect national boundaries. The art, music, poetry and philosophy which flowered with the great European universities such as Heidelberg, Oxford and Bologna were fostered by scholars who were at home in any European country.

The links amongst member states are still numerous. There is a common history, a Christian heritage, democratic systems, similar lifestyles and work ethics. It would be argued that the enlargement of the EC may dilute these common factors by admitting countries with non-Christian backgrounds or without a history of liberal democracy. But it could equally be argued that these countries will enrich the EC's culture rather than dilute it. And, in a primarily *economic* community, does any of this matter? Those who favour widening rather than deepening would surely argue it doesn't.

There is much talk of a youth culture in Europe which transcends national boundaries and which is built on popular music, fashion and the media. Encouraged by the growth of telecommunications, it is a phenomenon which could well spread with the potential enlargement of the EC. It is a potential catalyst for positive growth and for increased unity in the EC. The Community is trying to promote mobility and cultural exchange among young people in particular, through its funding of exchange and language schemes such as Erasmus, Petra and Comett. Perhaps the younger generation will be more receptive to the idea of a European culture.

Businesses have long since 'thought European' and identified European customers. The profile of such customers focuses on factors such as age, socio-economic group, income, attitudes, preferences and buying habits: nationality is a minor consideration. Brands such as Benetton and Swatch sit easily on the youth of all member states, as do the computer games they use, the trainers they wear and the soft drinks they consume. The global marketing machines of US and Japanese multinationals have long since targeted a European customer.

There are no easy answers to whether a pan-European culture either exists or is desirable; or whether the enlargement of the EC will encourage or discourage such a phenomenon. What is certain is that European culture has been admired and envied in many parts of the world for centuries and that Europe should be proud of its richness and diversity, promoting this wealth and using it to unify rather than divide.

What future for EMU?

At the beginning of this chapter, economic and monetary union was given as an example of an area of EC activity in which predictions might be made with relative confidence, as forward plans for its achievement have already been set out in some detail. However, debate continues on many aspects of the policy, including:

- whether the Exchange Rate Mechanism can survive in the face of currency market speculation

- the actual and desirable role of the German Bundesbank

- the likely benefits or costs to member states of participation in the ERM and the pursuit of the convergence criteria necessary for participation in EMU.

Is the ERM sustainable?

On the ERM see
chapter 7

The problems that beset the European Exchange Rate Mechanism during the latter half of 1992, and which forced the UK to withdraw from it, demonstrated to the EC that if international financial currency speculators applied concerted pressure to a particular member state's currency, then the EC would be powerless in its attempts to maintain that currency within its prescribed band.

THE ERM: THE CASE IN FAVOUR

- In the medium to long term (up to 1999) it will lead to the convergence of member states' interest rates at levels lower than those of the early 1990s
- This in turn will encourage investment in many sectors throughout the EC, with a consequent favourable impact on unemployment levels
- The situation of the early 1990s, with falling GNP and rising unemployment in many member states, demonstrates that the discipline of the ERM and eventually EMU is the only way forward; there is no credible alternative

THE ERM: THE CASE AGAINST

- The ERM and EMU will make existing problems worse, not better
- The convergence criteria that have to be met in order for countries to progress to Stage Three of EMU will force some states to deflate their national economies
- History shows that any pegged exchange rate system, such as the ERM, is fundamentally flawed and in the long term will destabilize the economies of its members
- There is no economic theory that states that the success of a single market depends on having a single currency. The practical example is cited of the North American Free Trade Agreement, in which a single currency has not even been suggested.

Some commentators believe that there is nothing inherently wrong with the theory underpinning the ERM (i.e. that it is possible to link the EC currencies together in the interests of international trade). It is argued that the problem began when the UK entered the system at a rate that was too high and could not be maintained, given the state of the UK economy; and that having realized this, the UK government should have realigned sterling in the ERM earlier. Other commentators believe that the crisis that befell the ERM during September and October 1992 was the result of a chance coming together of a set of circumstances that is very unlikely to be repeated in the future, in particular the state of the UK economy and the rejection of the Maastricht Treaty by the Danish in the first referedum.

Lessons were learnt, and policies in the future may reflect this learning process. The role of the German Bundesbank in the September/October 1992 ERM crisis was at the centre of much debate and it is likely that in the future both the European and the German authorities may consider factors beyond those of strictly economic relevance in determining its actions. Member states were also taught the salutary lesson that they could not rely on Germany automatically lowering its interest rates in order to bail them out of problems of their own making. The question was asked: what would replace the ERM should it collapse and what would the changes for the long-term success of EMU be without it? The box sets out the main arguments for and against the continuance of moves towards EMU and the maintenance of the ERM. Those on the middle ground, whilst accepting that the ERM is far from perfect, believe that it has been tested and, despite its faults, is workable. They hope that the latter half of the 1990s will see far fewer member states either 'temporarily withdrawing' or realigning their currencies, and that the ERM will succeed in its key purpose of reducing the fluctuations between members' currencies, which in turn will stimulate economic growth.

It may well be that the ground rules governing the current and future operation of EMU will have to be revised in order the address some of the criticisms levelled at it. A debate has begun as to whether or not the current convergence criteria for Stage 3 of EMU are too strict. Some argue that the permitted size of member state public sector deficits should be set at a higher rate. Others argue that some calculations should be removed from the criteria altogether in order that member states do not have to deflate just prior to Stage 3 but are able to use fiscal policies in a more flexible manner to 'fine-tune' their domestic economies.

The determining factor in the success or failure of the ERM may, however, be the operation of the single European market. It should provide the impetus which is needed for economic integration and convergence. If it does so, that will make the goal of economic and monetary union in the European Community achievable by the designated year of 1999.

Environmental Issues

One of the main areas of concern for the EC after Maastricht will be the cleaning up of an already dirty Europe and the prevention of further deterioration in the quality of the environment.

Figure 10 Wreckage of the tanker Braer, off the Shetland coast, January 1993
Source: *Topham*

The completion of the single market in January 1993 coincided with two reminders that environmental dangers know no frontiers with the disastrous wrecks of two oil tankers: the *Braer* off the coast of Shetland and the *Aegean Sea* off Spain.

The Maastricht Treaty explicitly includes among the objectives of the Community:

- preserving, protecting and improving the environment
- the prudent use of natural resources
- increased international cooperation to deal with environmental problems.

The Community already has in the pipeline 19 tough new Directives on environmental impacts, focusing on

- waste control
- emission control
- water quality.

The 'waste mountain'

Together the EC member states currently produce some 2.1 billion tonnes of waste per year, much of which is disposed of in an ever-increasing number of landfill sites. Already the Commission has put forward a plan that would force industry to recover 90% of its packaging; further Directives on recyclable packaging standards are likely to harmonize disparate national practices.

Germany has already introduced a scheme to tackle waste packaging: called 'Der Grüne Punkt' – the 'Green Dot Scheme' – it could serve as a model for a European waste recycling policy. Under this scheme, retailers are required to take back from customers all packaging materials, which must then be collected and disposed of by manufacturers. This obviously provides a strong incentive for manufacturers to reduce the amount of unnecessary packaging they generate in the first place.

Some companies, too, have taken initiatives to recycle both energy and products in an effort to reduce waste, cut costs and present an environmentally friendly face to the world. Again in Germany, Volkswagen at its Wolfsburg factory aims to be able to recycle many components of its cars in the future.

CFCs and the ozone layer

The production and consumption of chlorofluorocarbons (CFCs) will be prohibited in the Community after 1995; some governments are imposing even shorter national deadlines, and all governments are trying to achieve an 85% cut in the production of CFCs by the end of 1994. Recent research on damage to the ozone layer across northern Europe has lent urgency to this strand of environmental policy.

The 'green corridor'

Other environmental developments that are likely to be completed in the 1990s include a large-scale project coordinated by the European Trust for

Natural and Cultural Wealth. This huge plan involves the creation of a so-called 'green corridor' running from Finland to the Mediterranean through the old military training grounds in Eastern Europe. These areas are the last untouched wildernesses on the continent, and the preservation of their unique wildlife habitats is seen as imperative.

Enforcement of standards

As ever, the strongest incentive to clean up has to be the cost of not doing so. The EC acts as both stick and carrot in encouraging or compelling member states to fulfil environmental standards set by the Community. In 1992 alone the European Investment Bank lent over £350 million to the newly privatized UK water companies to enhance the quality and security of the water supply.

Meanwhile, Friends of the Earth have instituted proceedings against the British government for its failure to make the Thames Water Authority, one of the new private water authorities, comply with EC drinking water standards. The legal provision for individuals to sue member states in the European Court of Justice for a failure to implement a Directive which results in loss to the individual may, if successfully used, galvanize many member states into action.

The UK government has also come under fire from the European Commission, which decreed that seven major British developments were environmentally unacceptable. The Commission has plans to extend the scope of its intervention beyond that of maintaining individual projects towards the supervision of national governments' plans, policies and programmes.

A conflict of purpose?

At some stage a conflict may threaten between the environmentalists' principle of *sustainable* development and Community policies to foster *economic* development. It will be a prime task of the Community in the 21st century to avoid a clash between these two priorities. The protection of the European environment will inevitably be a matter of international cooperation or ultimately for supragovernmental enforcement, and the Community is well placed to exercise these responsibilities.

Useful addresses

EC institutions

Commission of the European Communities
200 rue de la Loi
1049 Bruxelles
Belgium
Tel. 010 322 235 111

The European Commission Information Office
8 Storey's Gate
London SW1P 3AT
Tel. 071 973 1992

The European Parliament Information Office
2 Queen Anne's Gate
London SW1H 9AA
Tel. 071 222 0411

British institutions

The British Overseas Trade Board
Department of Trade and Industry
Kingsgate House
66–74 Victoria Street
London SW1E 6SW
Tel. 0800 500 200

The Central Bureau for Educational Visits and Exchanges
Seymour Mews House
Seymour Mews
London W1H 9PE
Tel. 071 486 5101

The Department of Trade and Industry
Ashdown House
123 Victoria Street
London SW1E 6RB
Tel. 071 215 5000

Check first that you know which department you want.
DTI Hotline 081 200 1992

European Information Association
(Publications officer: Barbara Vickery)
Hallward Library
University of Nottingham
Nottingham NG7 2RD
Tel. 0602 484848

Institute of Export
64 Clifton Street
London EC2
Tel. 071 247 9812

Trade statistics

The Trade Statistics (Intrastat) Authority has an office in each member
state; their addresses follow.

Belgium
Trade Statistics (Intrastat) Authority
Institut National de Statistique/Nationaal Institut voor de Statistiek
Rue de Louvain 44/Leuvensweg 44
1000 Bruxelles/Brussel

Denmark
Trade Statistics (Intrastat) Authority
Danmarks Statistik
Sejrogade 11
DK–2100 Copenhagen

France
Trade Statistics (Intrastat) Authority
DG Douanes, Bureau des Statistiques
8 rue de la Tour des Dames
75009 Paris

Germany
Trade Statistics (Intrastat) Authority
Statistisches Bundesamt
Gustav-Stresemann-Ring 11
6200 Wiesbaden

Greece
Trade Statistics (Intrastat) Authority
National Statistical Officer of Greece
Lycourgou 14–16
101 66 Athens

Ireland
Trade Statistics (Intrastat) Authority
Central Statistics Office
St Stephen's Green House
Earlsfort Terrace
Dublin 2

Italy
Trade Statistics (Intrastat) Authority
Dipartimento Dogane–Minfinanze
Via M Carucci 85
Rome

Luxembourg
Trade Statistics (Intrastat) Authority
STATEC
19–21 Bd Royal
L–2013 Luxembourg

Netherlands
Trade Statistics (Intrastat) Authority
CBS
Kloosterweg 1
6401 CZ Heerlen

Portugal
Trade Statistics (Intrastat) Authority
Instituto Naçional de Estatistica
Av Antonio José de Almeida 5
1078 CODEX
Lisbon

Spain
Trade Statisatics (Intrastat) Authority
Departamento de Informatica Tributaria
Santa Maria Magdalena 16
28071 Madrid

UK
Trade Statistics (Intrastat) Authority
Intrastat Registration
Tariff & Statistical Office
HM Customs & Excise
CE Heath House
61 Victoria Avenue
Southend-on-Sea
Essex SS2 6EY

Glossary

ACP states	African, Caribbean and Pacific States who are parties to the Lomé Convention
block exemption	an exemption from competition rules contained in Article 85(3) of the Treaty of Rome
cabotage	the use of lorries registered in one country to carry goods in another
CAP	Common Agricultural Policy
CCT	Common Customs Tariff
CET	Common External Tariff
CFI	Court of First Instance
CFP	Common Fisheries Policy
COREPER	The Commitee of Permanent Representatives
cohesion	a policy of the EC to improve the economic and social aspects of underdeveloped areas in the community
Directive	a form of secondary Community law which must be enacted in a member state but which leaves the member state a degree of discretion as to the method in which the result of the directive must be achieved
directly applicable	Community rule such as a regulation which automatically becomes part of the domestic law of a member state
directly effective	Community law which gives a right to an individual enforceable in a national court
ECJ	European Court of Justice
ECSC	European Coal and Steel Community
ECU	European Currency Unit
EFTA	European Free Trade Association

EIB	European Investment Bank
EMS	European Monetary System
EPU	European Political Union
ERM	Exchange Rate Mechanism
ESC	Economic and Social Committee
ESF	European Social Fund
Euratom	European Atomic Energy Community
four freedoms	free movement of services, capital, goods and labour throughout the Community
GATT	General Agreement on Tariffs and Trade
IMF	International Monetary Fund
Lomé Convention	periodically updated agreement between the EC and the ACP giving trade preferences to the ACP states
OECD	Organization for Economic Cooperation and Development
proportionality	the concept that any measure used should not exceed that which is appropriate to achieve the required outcome
Regulation	a form of secondary regulation which is directly applicable in member states
SAD	Single Administrative Document
SEA	Single European Act
UKREP	British Embassy to the EC
WEU	Western European Union

Index